To my mother
Florence Palmer Copeland

Contents

Introduction

During her forty-two year career as a writer, Gertrude Stein produced some five-hundred-thirty-four titles, including novels, poems, plays, portraits, and articles in periodicals.[1] Yet, until recently, many educated Americans — even those educated in American literature — probably could associate her name only with *Three Lives, The Autobiography of Alice B. Toklas,* and "A rose is a rose is a rose." Many were astonished to learn that she had written anything else.

There is some indication that this situation is finally beginning to change. The year 1973 alone saw publication of at least three new works bringing together previously uncollected writings by Stein, and the reissuing of several previously published works, in paperback. Some new biographies also appeared. All this sudden activity amounts to a renaissance of interest in Stein.

For the neglect of Gertrude Stein as a serious artist, there is an explanation, if not a justification. She was a highly *experimental* writer who was not interested in writing "entertainments" (to use Graham Greene's term), but rather in creating something new. The use of the word "experiment" outside of the sciences could be problematic, but I have felt free to use the word throughout this book because Stein herself referred at least to some of her efforts with this term. In "Poetry and Grammar," contained in *Lectures in America* (p. 230), for example, she says:

> The vocabulary in prose is of course important if you like vocabulary is always important, in fact one of the things that you can find out and that I *experimented* with a great deal in How to Write vocabulary in itself and by itself can be interesting and can make sense. [Italics mine]

The point here is that Gertrude Stein expended a great deal of effort to wrest from the English language new realities. The word "experimentation" is used throughout this book to describe those wrestings.

She assessed the neglect of her own works in the following words:

> You see it is the people who generally smell of the museums who are accepted, and it is the new who are not accepted. You have got to accept a complete difference. It is hard to accept that, it is much easier to have one hand in the past. That is why James Joyce was accepted and I was not. He leaned toward the past, in my work the newness and difference is fundamental.[2]

The critics who did not accept the "new" in Stein's writings often dealt with her in derision and contempt. One whole camp of this kind of critical response can be represented by something Sinclair Lewis wrote about Stein in *Esquire* (July 1945):

> . . . When the exhibitionist deliberately makes his rites as confusing as possible, he is permitted to go on only because so many people are afraid to blurt out, 'I don't know what it

2

means.' For the same reason, Gertrude Stein, the Mother Superior of all that shoddy magic, is still extensively admired even though she is also extensively unread.[3]

Other critics were more perceptive. William Carlos Williams, for example, saw in Gertrude Stein's work the "imaginative quality" of Laurence Sterne's *The Life and Opinions of Tristram Shandy*. Williams wrote:

> The handling of the words ... is a direct forerunner of that which Gertrude Stein has woven today into a synthesis of its own. It will be plain, in fact, on close attention, that Sterne exercises not only the play (or music) of sight, sense and sound contrast among the words themselves which Stein uses, but their grammatical play also —.[4]

He continues: "Why in fact have we not heard more generally from American scholars upon the writings of Miss Stein? Is it lack of heart or ability or just that theirs is an enthusiasm which fades rapidly of its own nature before the risks of today?"[5]

Another writer who found serious intent in the works of Stein was her long-time friend Sherwood Anderson. He wrote:

> For me the work of Gertrude Stein consists in a rebuilding, an entire new recasting of life, in the city of words. Here is one artist who has been able to accept ridicule, ... to go live among the little housekeeping words, the swaggering bullying street-corner words, the honest working, money saving words, and all the other forgotten and neglected citizens of the sacred and half forgotten city.
>
> Would it not be a lovely and charmingly ironic gesture of the gods, in the end, if the work of this artist were to prove the most lasting and important of all the word slingers of our generation![6]

In more recent times there have been three very useful biographies of Stein's works.[7] While these works contain much valuable material, they suffer from the defects inherent in such a vast undertaking as the attempt to discuss everything she ever wrote — with little or no focus.

An attempt to bring into focus one aspect of Gertrude Stein's experimentation, and to trace that through her long writing career is the primary purpose of this study. Her use of the narrator has been selected for examination here because the role of the narrator changes with each phase of her experimentation. Stein herself referred to phases, or divisions, in her interest as a writer. In *Everybody's Autobiography*, for example, she said, ". . . my middle writing was painting,"[8] thereby suggesting that an investigation of her career might well be divided into three sections: the early years, the middle years, and the later years. Such an approach, indicated by Stein herself, seems not only logical but, as we will discover, inevitable.

Of course any investigation such as this one cannot be exhaustive; it will be, naturally, selective. Furthermore, the works discussed here are the ones from each period that seem to me to be representative of the experimentation in that period. Other investigators might choose other works that point to the same conclusions.

One further point needs clarification. Generally speaking, when a critic discusses the narrator in a work written by a man, the critic refers to that narrator as "he" without giving the matter another thought. (Of course I am not referring to works such as *Moll Flanders* in which the narrator has been identified as a woman.) In works written by men, in which the narrator has been given no particularized identity, the critic feels confident that his use of "he" to refer to the narrator will not act to confuse the narrator's identity with that of the man who wrote the work. But what happens when a woman writes a book? How does the critic refer to the narrator of, say, a Jane Austen work? (Who is the narrator of *Pride and Prejudice*, for example?) Do we refer to that narrator as "he," or as "she"? We are faced with the irony that the question should be irrelevant, but that the answer to it is not. If the English language included a singular form of "they" which did not allude to any gender (as languages such as Farsi, and Arabic do, for example), the problem of maintaining the distance between the narrator and the author of a work written by a woman would not arise. Unfortunately English grammar does not afford such a pronoun. The only form in English which has some acceptance at least as a quasi indefinite pronoun is "he" (as in the case of a referent to such indefinite nouns as "person"). The problem can be more easily appreciated if one imagines what would happen if one used "she" to refer to all unidentified narrators who appear in works written by women. Because we have not yet reached the point in our language where "she" carries the same indefinite application to all genders as "he" can, the use of "she" would draw attention to the author, therefore confusing the very distance we are trying to maintain. It is for this reason, therefore, that all of Stein's narrators in this study will be referred to as "he," except, of course, in such cases as *The Autobiography of Alice B. Toklas*, and *Everybody's Autobiography*, in which the narrator is clearly a woman. The use of "he" to refer to a narrator, then, is not meant to imply that that narrator is a man, but, rather, that

that narrator is some indefinite person not to be confused with the woman who wrote the work.

The final point to be made by way of introduction is that I am convinced that as Gertrude Stein's interests as an artist changed, she shifted from one kind of narrative technique to another which would allow her to reflect that change in interest. I hope that this study of the changes in her narrative technique will serve not only to illuminate her artistry, but also to provide some continuity to the experiments she spent her adult life making.

NOTES

1 Most of these titles have been catalogued. See Robert Haas and Donald Gallup, *A Catalogue of the Published and Unpublished Writings of Gertrude Stein* (New Haven: Yale University Press, 1941).

2 Gertrude Stein, "A Transatlantic Interview," in *Gertrude Stein, A Primer for the Gradual Understanding of Gertrude Stein,* ed. Robert Bartlett Haas (Los Angeles: Black Sparrow Press, 1971), p. 29.

3 Quoted by Robert Haas in Stein, "A Transatlantic Interview," p. 32. Immediately following Lewis's remarks, Gertrude Stein's answer to the charge appears, as follows:

> The facts of the case are that . . . most of us spent thirty years of our life in being made fun of and laughed at and criticized and having no existence and being without one cent of income. The work needs concentration, and one is often exhausted by it. No one would do this merely for exhibitionism; there is too much bitterness.

4 William Carlos Williams, *The Autobiography of William Carlos Williams* (New York: Random House, 1951), p. 256. Williams is referring here to an article he had written on Stein which was first published in *A Novelette and Other Prose, 1921-1931* (Toulon: F. Casson, 1932).

5 Williams, p. 255.

6 Sherwood Anderson, "Preface," in *Geography and Plays* by Gertrude Stein (Boston: The Four Seas, 1922), quoted in Ray Lewis White, ed., *Sherwood Anderson/Gertrude Stein, Correspondence and Personal Essays* (Chapel Hill: University of North Carolina Press, 1972), p. 17.

7 Donald Sutherland, *Gertrude Stein: A Biography of Her Work* (New Haven: Yale University Press, 1951); Richard Bridgman, *Gertrude Stein in Pieces* (New York: Oxford University Press, 1970); John Malcolm Brinnin, *The Third Rose: Gertrude Stein and Her World* (Boston: Little, Brown, 1959).

8 Gertrude Stein, *Everybody's Autobiography* (New York: Random House, 1937), p. 180.

The Early Years: 1903-1912

QUOD ERAT DEMONSTRANDUM

Largely because of the "newness" and the "difference" in Gertrude Stein's works she had great difficulty all her life with public as well as critical acceptance. Many of her works, therefore, were published long after they were completed. This often results in some difficulty in determining exactly when any particular work of hers was written.[1]

That *Quod Erat Demonstrandum*[2] was certainly finished by 1903 has been established by Leon Katz,[3] and by Donald Gallup.[4] But the work was not published until 1950 — four years after Stein's death, and forty-seven years after it was written.

Another problem with this work is that it has two titles. The one that Stein gave to it is *Quod Erat Demonstrandum*. But, when the work was first published (posthumously), her executors changed the title, using a phrase from the end of the book, and published it under the title *Things As They Are*.[5] It was not until 1971 that the work was reissued by Leon Katz under its original title. Therefore all references to the work in this book will be to the 1971 edition, which is the original title and text.

There is, however, a problem with the work which goes beyond the problems of dates and editions. Most scholars have accepted the questionable testimony that Gertrude Stein "forgot" the manuscript of *Q.E.D.* for many years after it was written. Scholars have cited as evidence for this "fact" the narrator's word in *The Autobiography of Alice B. Toklas.* The narrator says:

> The funny thing about this short novel is that she completely forgot about it for many years. She remembered beginning a little later writing the Three Lives but this first piece of writing was completely forgotten, she had never mentioned it to me, even when I first knew her. She must have forgotten about it almost immediately.[6]

As we will discover later, in the section dealing with *The Autobiography of Alice B. Toklas,* Gertrude Stein is the *author* of this book — not the *narrator.* The critics who have fallen into the trap of confusing Stein's voice with Toklas's voice in this book[7] are confusing the "implied author"[8] with what, after all, amounts to a character in a book by that author.

It is, moreover, entirely possible that Alice Toklas (the *narrator* of the "Autobiography") really did not know the *Q.E.D.* manuscript still existed, while Gertrude Stein (the *author* of the "Autobiography") had not for a moment forgotten it. This possibility seems very strong because of the subject matter of *Q.E.D.* Katz writes in his "Introduction," "Before Stein left America in 1903 for her permanent stay in Europe, she had been living through an agonizing love affair which is recounted in minute and accurate detail in

Q.E.D., her first complete novel" (iii). He further states that the love affair was with May Bookstaver, a fellow student of Gertrude Stein's at Johns Hopkins.

The story of *Q.E.D.* involves a homosexual triangle. It is quite possible that Gertrude Stein simply did not choose to show this material to Alice Toklas,[9] the woman who had replaced May Bookstaver. The importance of the point to this discussion is that it can be proved that Stein certainly did not "forget" this early work, since she carefully copied its structure and plot elements in the "Melanctha" story of *Three Lives*. (Stein changed the homosexual elements to heterosexual ones for "Melanctha," of course, but there are some thirty-four parallels in plot and dialogue between the two works. Some of the parallels are so close that it makes the idea that she forgot the work impossible to believe.)[10] The importance of this point to any study of the development of Stein's use of narrative techniques becomes obvious. She used the same materials and produced two dramatically different works — because she applied two radically different narrative techniques to those materials.

With the exception of its subject matter, *Quod Erat Demonstrandum* is the most conventional work that Gertrude Stein ever wrote. It has a plot, characters, a narrator, a beginning, a middle, and an end. It also shows an early indebtedness to Henry James — in spite of the narrator's statements to the contrary in *The Autobiography of Alice B. Toklas* (which, again, some critics have taken to be Gertrude Stein's statements). The narrator of the "Autobiography" says that while Stein greatly admired William James (who was a teacher of hers at Radcliffe), she "was not then at all interested in the works of Henry James" (96). The narrator then adds,

> In the same way she contends that Henry James was the first person in literature to find the way to the literary methods of the twentieth century. But oddly enough in all of her formative period she did not read him and was not interested in him. But as she often says one is always naturally antagonistic to one's parents and sympathetic to one's grandparents. The parents are too close, they hamper you, one must be alone. So perhaps that is the reason why only very lately Gertrude Stein reads Henry James. [96-97]

This statement is simply not true. Not only did Gertrude Stein read Henry James at least as early as 1903 when she wrote *Q.E.D.*, but she admired his writing enough to emulate his use of the central intelligence in *Q.E.D.*, and to quote directly from *The Wings of the Dove* (first published in 1902). Moreover, Stein refers to Kate Croy by name in *Q.E.D.*

The following excerpt is from *Wings of the Dove* (Kate Croy is speaking to Merton Densher): "I *shan't* sacrifice you . . . I shall sacrifice nobody and nothing, and that's just my situation, that I want and that I shall try for everything."[11]

This is from Stein's *Q.E.D.* (written the following year): " 'What a condemned little prostitute it is,' Adele said to herself between a laugh and a groan. 'I know there is no use in asking for an explanation. Like Kate Croy she would tell me "I shall sacrifice nothing and nobody" and that's just her situation, she wants and will try for everything' " (121).

Once again, accusing Stein of falsifying the facts in *The Autobiography of Alice B. Toklas* is not the point here. To say that would be to fall into the same trap as

11

those who believe that every word the narrator says is the "truth" from the mouth of Gertrude Stein. The point is raised only because some early Jamesian influences in Stein's writings are apparent, and it seems necessary to demonstrate that the narrator of *The Autobiography of Alice B. Toklas* should not be considered a final authority on matters of this kind.[12]

Q.E.D. is related by a third-person, omniscient narrator, quite conventionally nineteenth-century, or earlier, in origin. When the central character, Adele, is on stage, so to speak, the narrator often switches to an examination of Adele's consciousness exclusively — unlike earlier third-person narration.

The work is divided into three chapters, each bearing the name of a different woman ("Adele," "Mabel Neathe," "Helen"). But, in the final analysis, Adele is the real central intelligence of all three chapters. In fact, throughout the work, Gertrude Stein is fluctuating between the influences of nineteenth-century narrative techniques, and those of the Jamesian central intelligence, more often associated with the twentieth century.

The following excerpt is offered as an example of the nineteenth-century omniscient narrator so often visible in *Q.E.D.*:

Mabel Neathe's room fully met the habit of many hours of unaggressive lounging. She had command of an exceptional talent for atmosphere. The room with its very good shape, dark walls but mediocre furnishings and decorations was more than successfully unobtrusive, it had perfect quality. It had always just the amount of light necessary to make mutual observation pleasant and yet to leave the decorations in obscurity or rather to inspire a faith in their being good.

It is true of rooms as of human beings that they are bound to have one good feature and as a Frenchwoman dresses to that feature in such fashion that the observer must see that and notice nothing else, so Mabel Neathe had arranged her room so that one enjoyed one's companions and observed consciously only the pleasant fire-place. [70]

The tendency of Stein's narrator to generalize about all of human experience is even more evident in another excerpt:

Modern situations never endure for a long enough time to allow subtle and elaborate methods to succeed. By the time they are beginning to bring about results the incident is forgotten. Subtlety moreover in order to command efficient power must be realised as dangerous and the modern world is a difficult place in which to be subtly dangerous, the risks are too great. Mabel might now compel by inspiring pity, she could never in her world compel by inspiring fear. [71-72]

What can be seen further from these two passages is that one of the narrative techniques in *Q.E.D.* is a narrator who not only knows everything, but can reach instructive conclusions for the edification of his reader based on all the knowledge in the universe, whether that knowledge is relevant to the work at hand or not. Such a technique is most often associated with the nineteenth century, or with an even earlier period.

Again, this is not the only narrative technique to be found in *Q.E.D.* Whenever Adele, the central character, enters the action the narrator becomes an entirely different essence. This point will be demonstrated shortly, but because Adele is *rendered* in this work, and not merely objectively described, as the other characters are, a brief summary of the plot may be helpful before continuing the discussion.

Essentially the story is about Adele, who becomes involved in a homosexual triangle. As Hoffman[13] has suggested, the story really is not "about" homosexuality at all. It is, rather, about two women who reach a hopeless "emotional impasse."[14] One of the women, Adele, grows through the experience to the point where she is able to see "things as they really are"; but the other one, Helen, does not. At the beginning of the story, Helen is involved in a homosexual liaison with Mabel. This liaison, as is slowly revealed through the plot, is predicated on Mabel's money, and Helen's lack of it. Helen is, in effect, being kept by Mabel. Into this setting arrives Adele, and the plot becomes an unfolding of Adele's growing attraction for Helen, and vice versa. However, Adele can love Helen only physically — she can never feel anything but profound disappointment with Helen's superficial values. The story ends with the two women being profoundly "out of rhythm"[15] with each other. Only Adele, of course, recognizes this.

While the work is divided into three chapters, each bearing the name of one of the women, the three segments are by no means handled in the same way by the narrator. Adele's is the only consciousness ever entered. Mabel's personality is summarized thus by the narrator, "Mabel's ancestry did not supply an explanation of her character. Her kinship with decadent Italy was purely spiritual" (71). Helen's character is also summarized:

> She was the American version of the English handsome girl. In her ideal completeness she would have been unaggressively determined, a trifle brutal and entirely impersonal; a woman of passions but not of emotions, capable of long sustained action, incapable of regrets. In this American edition it amounted at its best to no more than a brave bluff. In the strength of her youth

> Helen still thought of herself as the unfrustrated ideal; she had
> as yet no suspicion of her weakness . . . . [54-55]

But Adele's personality gets no such objective summa-
tion by the narrator. Adele speaks for herself:

> I probably have the experience of all apostles, I am rejected by
> the class whose cause I preach but that has nothing to do with
> the case. I simply contend that the middle-class ideal which de-
> mands that people be affectionate, respectable, honest and con-
> tent, that they avoid excitements and cultivate serenity is the
> ideal that appeals to me, it is in short the ideal of affectionate
> family life, of honorable business methods. [59]

By the time the book progresses to the third chapter,
the one supposedly dealing with Helen, Adele has
become so much the central intelligence that the whole
of Helen's chapter is seen through Adele's eyes. Such
has not been the narrator's method previously. The
book ends with a scene in which Adele is alone "on
stage." And, by this time, the highly obtrusive narrator
of the first half of the book has become subordinated to
Adele's intelligence,[16] and the book ends with the
almost total disappearance of that narrator:

> Adele read the letter impatiently. 'Hasn't she yet learned that
> things do happen and she isn't big enough to stave them off'
> she exclaimed. 'Can't she see things as they are and not as she
> would make them if she were strong enough as she plainly isn't.
> I am afraid it comes very near being a dead-lock,' she groaned
> dropping her head on her arms. [133]

What can be seen in Stein's earliest work, then, is
that she fluctuated between the obtrusive third-person
narrator of the nineteenth century, and the much less
obtrusive third-person narrator who examines closely a
single, central intelligence. She was never to show
quite the same indecision again in her work, even

though much of the later work is primarily experimental.

THREE LIVES

Between the writing of *Q.E.D.* and her next important work, *Three Lives*,[17] Gertrude Stein undertook the task of translating Gustave Flaubert's *Trois Contes*. She found many elements in one of these three stories, "Un Coeur Simple," ("A Simple Soul") which were to play a large part in her development as an artist. She wrote many years later:

> Everything I have done has been influenced by Flaubert and Cézanne, and this gave me a new feeling about composition. Up to that time composition had consisted of a central idea, to which everything else was an accompaniment and separate but was not an end in itself, and Cézanne conceived the idea that in composition one thing was as important as another thing. Each part is as important as the whole, and that impressed me enormously, and it impressed me so much that I began to write *Three Lives* under this influence . . . .[18]

Stein never exactly says what elements in Flaubert influenced her, but they can easily be traced. First, a brief examination of some of the elements to be found in "A Simple Soul" is necessary.

This story was especially important to Stein in the writing of two of the three stories of *Three Lives:* "The Good Anna," and "The Gentle Lena." The other story from *Three Lives*, "Melanctha," was, as has been noted, a reworking of materials from *Q.E.D.*, and so requires special consideration in this discussion. "Melanctha" was broadly influenced by Flaubert, to be sure, but since "The Good Anna," and "The Gentle Lena" were influenced in particular by plot elements and characterizations found in "A Simple Soul," as "Melanctha" was not, "The Good Anna," and "The Gentle Lena" should receive attention first.

Briefly, Flaubert's "A Simple Soul" is about the life of a servant, Félicité, "of limited intelligence."[19] She is employed for fifty years by a Madame Aubain, an egocentric widow with two children, Virginia and Paul. Félicité, in her youth, had had a brief and chaste love affair with a boy who had deserted her to marry a rich widow, following which she was employed by Madame Aubain. As the story progresses, Madame Aubain's little girl, Virginia, whom both Madame Aubain and Félicité love, dies and the mother is disconsolate. Then Félicité has a similar experience. Her young nephew dies. She had idolized him although he thought little more of her than as a source of money. A neighbor, who had been a consul in America, gives Madame Aubain a parrot. Félicité longs to have it because it reminds her of her nephew who died in America. Madame Aubain gives the parrot to Félicité, and she teaches it to say a few words. When the bird dies, Félicité has it stuffed: it has become a symbol to her of all that she ever loved in a lonely world. The bird is described at Félicité's death:

> A blue vapor arose in Félicité's room. She opened her nostrils and inhaled it with a mystic sensuousness; then she closed her lids. Her lips smiled. The beats of her heart grew fainter and fainter, and vaguer, like a fountain giving out, like an echo dying away; — and when she exhaled her last breath she thought she saw in the half-opened heavens a gigantic parrot hovering above her head. [328]

The story is told by a third-person narrator who is almost invisible, as can be seen in the short passage

17

quoted above. This narrator, though omniscient, tells the story from the point of view of Félicité only. However, we never enter the mind of Félicité — the point of view remains entirely outside. The narrator's "voice" is very low-keyed throughout the story, low-keyed and without hope, as the story itself is. Neither the life nor the death of the simple servant evokes the slightest emotion from the narrator.

Because this is an important element in the discussion of *Three Lives,* just what Flaubert has done with this impassive narrator should be examined.

In *Axel's Castle,* Edmund Wilson discusses the reaction that took place in the nineteenth century against what he terms, "the sentimentality, and the looseness of Romanticism."[20] He sees the group of poets who immediately preceded Flaubert as the precursors of the impassive narration which was a product of this reaction.

> The Parnassian group of poets, who made their first appearance in the fifties — Gautier, Leconte de Lisle, Heredia — seemed to have taken it for their aim merely to picture historical incidents and natural phenomena as objectively and accurately as possible in impassive perfect verse. [7]

Writers like Gustave Flaubert, who came after the Parnassian group of poets, consciously stripped Romantic sentimentality from the voice of their narration. This is not to suggest, of course, that their narrators are completely objective for, as Wayne Booth[21] has pointed out, complete objectivity is impossible. But what Flaubert has done in "A Simple Soul" is to present a narrator who judiciously attempts to speak "objectively" about his characters.

We have seen that Gertrude Stein's narrative techniques in *Q.E.D.* were a combination of the obtrusive nineteenth-century omniscient narrator and the narrator who focuses on the inner life of one central intelligence. When she had completed *Q.E.D.* (and had a few sketches done in the same manner — "Fernhurst" and the early chapters of *The Making of Americans*),[22] she began writing three stories that evidenced a dramatic change in narrative techniques. Gone completely from these stories is the obtrusive narrator of *Q.E.D.* And gone, at least for the moment, is the focus on any inner life of the central intelligence. As will be demonstrated directly, the narrator of *Three Lives* has the same low-keyed voice without emotion as the narrator of "A Simple Soul." And gone are the little essays, so prevalent in *Q.E.D.*, in which the narrator appears to have unlimited knowledge of all human behavior. In short, the narrator of *Three Lives* becomes much more controlled artistically than the narrator of *Q.E.D.*, although Stein did add to her narrator a dimension of her own which was absent in Flaubert.

"The Good Anna," the first story in *Three Lives*, bears the closest resemblance in plot elements to "A Simple Soul." Anna is a servant girl; she works for an egocentric mistress who has two young wards; and she even has a parrot (although the parrot has no real bearing on the plot.) Both Félicité and Anna are entirely dominated by women all their lives. Flaubert describes Félicité: "Her face was thin and her voice shrill. When she was twenty-five, she looked forty. After she had passed fifty, nobody could tell her age; erect and silent always, she resembled a wooden figure working automatically" (307). Stein says of Anna: "The good Anna was a small, spare, german [*sic*] woman, at this time about forty years of age. Her face was worn, her cheeks were thin, her mouth drawn and firm, and her light blue eyes were very bright. Sometimes they were full of lightning and sometimes full of humor, but they were always sharp and clear" (13).

Compare the short, factual sentences, and the objectivity of Flaubert and the Stein of "The Good Anna," above, with the following passage of narration written by Stein in *Q.E.D.*:

> As Mabel Neathe lay on the deck . . ., her attitude of awkward discomfort and the tension of her long angular body sufficiently betrayed her New England origin. It is one of the peculiarities of American womanhood that the body of a coquette often encloses the soul of a prude and the angular form of a spinster is possessed by a nature of the tropics.[55]

The change in narrative technique between *Q.E.D.* and "The Good Anna" is nowhere more dramatically in evidence than at Anna's death: "In a few days they had Anna ready. Then they did the operation, and then the Good Anna with her strong, strained, worn-out body died" (82). That such objectivity is one of the lessons Stein learned from Flaubert ˙ unmistakable. The following is from "A Simple Soul":

> A long while afterward [Félicité] learned through Victor's captain, the circumstances which surrounded his death. At the hospital they had bled him too much, treating him for yellow fever. Four doctors held him at one time. He died almost instantly, ... [317]

A brief look at "The Gentle Lena," from *Three Lives*, reveals further evidence of Flaubert's influences. Lena is another servant girl, but she is much closer to the actual characterization of Félicité than was Anna. While the good Anna attempts to organize, and to "take charge" of her mistress' life (18), poor gentle Lena is "too stupid" (252) to be anything but *acted upon* in her life. She is described at the opening of the story: "Lena was patient, gentle, sweet and german" (239). She goes through life doing whatever anyone tells her to do until, finally, she is married by someone else's edict, and always she works very hard. The narrator of this story presents Lena's passivity (note the passivity in the narrator's voice) as follows:

> The good cook sometimes made Lena come to see her. Lena would come with her baby and sit there in the kitchen, and watch the good woman cooking, and listen to her sometimes a little, the way she used to, while the good german woman scolded her for going around looking so careless when now she had no trouble, and sitting there so dull, and always being just so thankless. Sometimes Lena would wake up a little and get back into her face her old, gentle, patient, and unsuffering sweetness, but mostly Lena did not seem to hear much when the good german woman scolded. . . . mostly Lena just lived along and was careless in her clothes, and dull, and lifeless. [277-78]

Flaubert's narrator is similarly passive when presenting Félicité's situations:

> Like every other woman, she had had an affair of the heart. Her father, who was a mason, was killed by falling from a scaffolding. Then her mother died and her sisters went their different ways; a farmer took her in, and while she was quite small, let her keep cows in the fields. She was clad in miserable rags, beaten for the slightest offence and finally dismissed for a theft of thirty sous which she did not commit. She took service on another farm where she tended the poultry; and as she was well thought of by her master, her fellow-workers soon grew jealous. [307]

That Stein had learned the short, impassive sentence

from Flaubert has already been demonstrated. But Lena's death scene is a minor triumph in the kind of controlled narration to which Flaubert's influence led Stein.

> Lena was always more and more lifeless and Herman now mostly never thought about her. He more and more took all the care of their three children. He saw to their eating right and their washing, and he dressed them every morning, and he taught them the right way to do things, and he put them to their sleeping, and he was now always every minute with them. Then there was to come to them, a fourth baby. Lena went to the hospital near by to have the baby. Lena seemed to be going to have much trouble with it. When the baby was come out at last, it was like its mother lifeless. While it was coming, Lena had grown very pale and sicker. When it was all over Lena had died, too, and nobody knew just how it had happened to her. [278-79]

It may seem that the narrative techniques Stein learned from translating Flaubert have been overemphasized here, but since these techniques are important in tracing Stein's further development as a writer, and since they have not been sufficently discussed by previous critics of her work,[23] perhaps the emphasis has been justified.

However, the narrators of "The Good Anna," and "The Gentle Lena," are no mere slavish imitations of Flaubert. It is true that both Stein's and Flaubert's narrators are impassive, and outside the minds of their characters. But Flaubert's distance is so much greater than Stein's that it constitutes a difference in kind. And this is Stein's great innovation in *Three Lives*: she enters the minds of her characters *without appearing to do so*. In fact, she is not, strictly speaking, inside their minds; but her narrator picks up their speech patterns and rhythms — thereby "sounding" like the characters themselves. Flaubert, on the other hand, always made a clear distinction between the narrator's voice and that of his characters. Stein's narrators appear to blend into the characters.

Lena's death scene is a good case in point. In the sentence, "Lena was always more and more lifeless and Herman now mostly never thought about her," any native speaker of English can recognize a special, unsyntactical use of the language. It is not a character in the story speaking, it is the narrator. The language is brilliantly arranged to pick up the passivity of Lena, and the impassivity of Herman, both Germans, living now in America. So, when the narrator joins these characters in their slightly "foreign" ways of phrasing things, the narrator appears to enter their thoughts, without actually doing so. It is a narrative technique which is very effective in rendering the narrator "invisible." Stein uses this technique throughout all three of the "Lives."

Edmund Wilson has summarized this innovative technique by Stein in his essay on her in *Axel's Castle*.[24] His analysis is marred, however, by his insistence (shared by many other critics) that "Melanctha" is mainly a perceptive story about Negroes. The entire passage is quoted below because it helps to summarize what has been said here about Stein's innovative technique in "The Good Anna," and "The Gentle Lena," and also because his remarks about "Melanctha," although, viewed herein as erroneous, present a logical springboard for the examination of that story.

What is most remarkable in these stories — especially if we

compare them with such a typically Naturalistic production as Flaubert's 'Un Coeur Simple,' in which we feel that the old family servant has been seen from a great distance and documented with effort — is the closeness with which the author has been able to identify herself with her characters. In a style which appears to owe nothing to that of any other novelist, she seems to have caught the very rhythms and accents of the minds of her heroines: we find ourselves sharing the lives of the Good Anna and Gentle Lena so intimately that we forget about their position and see the world limited to their range, just as in Melanctha's case — and this is what makes her story one of the best as well as one of the earliest attempts of a white American novelist to understand the mind of the modern Americanized negro — we become so immersed in Melanctha's world that we quite forget its inhabitants are black and we discover that these histories have a significant difference from that of ordinary realistic fiction: Miss Stein is interested in her subjects, not from the point of view of the social conditions of which they might be taken as representative, but as three fundamental types of women. ... Behind the limpid and slightly monotonous simplicity of Gertrude Stein's sentences, one becomes aware of her masterly grasp of the organisms, contradictory and indissoluble which human personalities are. [237-38]

One consideration must be handled immediately: "Melanctha" is not really a story about the ethnic reality of Negroes.[25] Indeed, it is the point of this discussion that "Melanctha" is a reworking of the materials of *Q.E.D.* Many critics, who, like Edmund Wilson, assumed that the characters are Negroes because the narrator says they are, did not have the advantage of having seen a copy of *Q.E.D.* before they wrote, since they wrote before the 1950 publication of that work. Of course, other critics wrote after 1950 and still made the same erroneous assumptions.[26]

It will be recalled that *Q.E.D.*, written in 1903, concerned three homosexual women involved in a triangle. When one considers the trouble Theodore Dreiser had with *Sister Carrie* during that same period, it is not surprising that Gertrude Stein dropped the homosexual elements from her story before using the material again. Some very important elements of *Q.E.D.*, however, would have become problematic in a simple shift from homosexual to heterosexual in the story, and these elements must be discussed briefly.

In *Q.E.D.* Adele and Helen together undergo a full and complete series of sexual experiences, and obviously they are not married when they experience them. It is important to Adele's full realization of how completely "out of rhythm" she and Helen are that they not be married. Adele must be able to walk away from the experience with no ties such as marriage to complicate it. At the turn of this century in America the only background against which a writer could portray premarital sexual relationships without having an outraged white, middle-class public to contend with was one dealing with Negroes. It was part of the white man's view of the black man that they were sexually promiscuous. If Gertrude Stein wished to drop the homosexual elements and make them heterosexual, her choice of Negroes instead of whites allowed her to retain as much as possible of the important extramarital elements involved. And this is exactly what she did.

The most important relationship in *Q.E.D.* is the one between Adele and Helen. In "Melanctha," this becomes the relationship between Dr. Jeff Campbell and Melanctha Herbert. In the following excerpts from the two works the parallels are unmistakable.

The first one is from Q.E.D. Adele is speaking to Helen and Mabel:

'Of course I am not logical,' she said 'logic is all foolishness. The whole duty of man consists in being reasonable and just . . . . I am reasonable because I know the difference between understanding and not understanding and I am just because I have no opinion about things I don't understand.'

To which Helen answers,

'That sounds very well indeed . . . but somehow I don't feel that your words really express you. Mabel tells me that you consider yourself a typical middle-class person, that you admire above all things the middle-class ideals and yet you certainly don't seem one in thoughts or opinions. When you show such a degree of inconsistency how can you expect to be believed?'

Adele then says,

'The contradiction isn't in me,' Adele said sitting up to the occasion and illustrating her argument by vigorous gestures, 'it is in your perverted ideas. You have a foolish notion that to be middle-class is to be vulgar, that to cherish the ideals of respectability and decency is to be commonplace and that to be the mother of children is to be low. You tell me that I am not middle-class and that I can believe in none of these things because I am not vulgar, commonplace and low, but it is just there where you make your mistake. You don't realise the important facts that virtue and vice have it in common that they are vulgar when not passionately given. You think that they carry within them a different power. Yes they do because they have different world-values, but as for their relation to vulgarity, it is as true of vice as of virtue that you can't sell what should be passionately given without forcing yourself into many acts of vulgarity and the chances are that in endeavoring to escape the vulgarity of virtue, you will find yourselves engulfed in the vulgarity of vice. Good gracious! here I am at it again. I never seem to know how to keep still, but you both know already that I have the failing of my tribe. I believe in the sacred rites of conversation even when it is a monologue.' [56-57]

The following is an exchange from "Melanctha." Note the similarities between the ideas of Adele and Dr. Campbell, and those of Helen and Melanctha.

Dr. Campbell soon got through with his reading, in the old newspapers, and then somehow he began to talk along about the things he was always thinking. Dr. Campbell said he wanted to work so that he could understand what troubled people, and not to just have excitements, and he believed you ought to love your father and your mother and to be regular in all your life, and not to be always wanting new things and excitements, and to always know where you were, and what you wanted, and to always tell everything just as you meant it. That's the only kind of life he knew or believed in, Jeff Campbell repeated. 'No I ain't got any use for all the time being in excitements and wanting to have all kinds of experience all the time. I got plenty of experience just living regular and quiet and with my family, and doing my work, and taking care of people, and trying to understand it. I don't believe much in this running around business and I don't want to see the colored people do it. I am a colored man and I ain't sorry, and I want to see the colored people like what is good and what I want them to have, and that's to live regular and work hard and understand things, and that's enough to keep any decent man excited.' [116-17]

To this Melanctha replies,

It don't seem to me Dr. Campbell, that what you say and what you do seem to have much to do with each other. And about your being so good Dr. Campbell. . . . You don't care about going to church much yourself, and yet you always are saying you believe so much in things like that, for people. It seems to me, Dr. Campbell you want to have a good time just like all us others, and then you just keep on saying that it's right to be good and you ought not to have excitements, and yet you really don't want to do it Dr. Campbell, no more than me. . . . No, Dr. Campbell, it certainly does seem to me you don't know very well yourself, what you mean, when you are talking. [117-18]

Dr. Campbell, then, is the same seeker of understanding and knowledge that Adele is. And Melanctha and Helen are the same troubled spirits.

Melanctha's youth is, for example, described by the narrator as follows:

> The young Melanctha did not love her father and her mother, and she had a break neck courage, and a tongue that could be very nasty. Then, too, Melanctha went to school and was very quick in all the learning, and she knew very well how to use this knowledge to annoy her parents who knew nothing.
>
> Melanctha Herbert had always had a break neck courage. Melanctha always loved to be with horses; she loved to do wild things, to ride the horses and to break and tame them. [91]

Helen's youth is similarly documented. Adele says to Mabel Neathe, ". . . but you know I really know very little about [Helen] except that she dislikes her parents and goes in for society a great deal. What else is there?" (73). The narrator then says,

> Mabel described their attempts to break Helen's spirit and their anger at their lack of success. 'And now,' Mable went on 'they object to everything she does. . . . Of course they are proud of her good looks, her cleverness and social success but she won't get married and she doesn't care to please the people her mother wants her to belong to. They don't dare to say anything to her now because she is so much better able to say things that hurt than they are.' . . . She then lauded Helen's courage and daring. 'Whenever there is any difficulty with the horses or anything dangerous to be done they always call in Helen. . . . Her courage never fails and that is what makes her father so bitter, that she never gives any sign of yielding and if she decides to do a thing she is perfectly reckless, nothing stops her.' [73-74]

One of the most striking parallels between Melanctha and Helen comes in an accident both girls suffered in their youths:

Mabel then described Helen's remarkable endurance of pain. She fell from a haystack one day and broke her arm. After she got home, her father was so angry that he wouldn't for some time have it attended to and she faced him boldly to the end. 'She never winces or complains no matter how much she is hurt. . . .' [*Q.E.D.*, 75]

Sometimes Melanctha would do some of these things that had much danger. . . . Once she slipped and fell from a high place. A workman caught her and so she was not killed, but her left arm was badly broken.
All the men crowded around her. They admired her boldness in doing and in bearing pain when her arm was broken. They all went along with her with great respect to the doctor, and then they took her home in triumph and all of them were bragging about her not squealing.
James Herbert was home where his wife lived, that day. He was furious when he saw the workmen and Melanctha. He drove the men away with curses . . . , and he would not let a doctor come in to attend Melanctha. [102-3]

Earlier it was mentioned that there are some thirty-four such parallels to be found between *Q.E.D.* and "Melanctha." It is very tempting to continue citing these parallels here merely to show that "Melanctha" is a reworking of the materials of *Q.E.D.* There is, however, a larger point under consideration — that in the reworking of these materials Stein's narrative techniques have undergone some major changes.

It has been seen in the other two stories from *Three Lives*, that Stein utilized the impassive, factual narrator, as well as some of the plot elements she found in "A Simple Soul." But it was also seen that she added to that impassive, objective voice the speech patterns and rhythms of her characters, and by so doing, created her own narrative technique.

This technique is brought to "Melanctha," along

with another method barely hinted at in "The Good Anna." This is the matter of deliberate narrative repetition, for which Gertrude Stein was to become famous, and in some quarters, infamous.

With these considerations in mind — the establishment of the parallels between *Q.E.D.* and "Melanctha" primarily to distinguish between the vastly differing narrative techniques used in the two works — the choice of parallels will be confined hereafter to those which demonstrate these differences.

Consider the differences in the narrative technique between the following two passages:

> There was a long silence and Adele looked observingly at the stars. Suddenly she felt herself intensely kissed on the eyes and on the lips. She felt vaguely that she was apathetically unresponsive. There was another silence. Helen looked steadily down at her. 'Well!' she brought out at last. 'Oh' began Adele slowly 'I was just thinking.' 'Haven't you every stopped thinking long enough to feel?' Helen questioned gravely. Adele shook her head in slow negation. 'Why I suppose if one can't think at the same time I will never accomplish the feat of feeling. I always think. I don't see how one can stop it. Thinking is a pretty continuous process' she continued 'sometimes it's more active than at others but it's always pretty much there.' [*Q.E.D.*, 66]

> Then they were again very silent, sitting there together, with the lamp between them, that was always smoking. Melanctha began to lean a little more toward Dr. Campbell, where he was sitting, and then she took his hand between her two and pressed it hard, but she said nothing to him. She let it go then and leaned a little nearer to him. Jefferson moved a little but did not do anything in answer. At last, 'Well,' said Melanctha sharply to him. 'I was just thinking' began Dr. Campbell slowly, 'I was just wondering,' he was beginning to get ready to go on with his talking. 'Don't you ever stop with your thinking long

enough ever to have any feeling Jeff Campbell,' said Melanctha a little sadly. 'I don't know,' said Jeff Campbell slowly, 'I don't know Miss Melanctha much about that. No, I don't stop thinking much Miss Melanctha and if I can't ever feel without stopping thinking, I certainly am very much afraid Miss Melanctha that I never will do much with that kind of feeling. Sure you ain't worried Miss Melanctha, about my really not feeling very much all the time. I certainly do think I feel some, Miss Melanctha, even though I always do it without ever knowing how to stop with my thinking.' ["Melanctha," 131-32]

The narrator in the first passage, quoted from *Q.E.D.*, has focused on the central intelligence, Adele. The action of the passage is seen through Adele's eyes, but the language used by the narrator calls the attention away from Adele so that the reader remains a distance from her. "She felt vaguely that she was apathetically unresponsive." The language jars, and by so doing, reminds the reader that a narrator is present, recording the scene. The same thing is true with phrases such as "Helen questioned gravely." Author intrusion is not present in the passage from "Melanctha." The language of the narrator here has taken on the personality of the characters involved. "Melanctha began to lean a little more toward Dr. Campbell, where he was sitting. . . ." The phrase, "where he was sitting," serves to focus the reader's attention on the couple, and on Melanctha's slow movement toward Jeff. The mood of Jeff's mind is captured unobtrusively by the narrator in "he was beginning to get ready to go on with his thinking." The narrator has captured Jeff's slow speech here, as well as Jeff's tendency to circumlocute, with this piece of narration which is itself circumlocution.

One additional comparison should suffice to make the point.

One night [Adele] was lying on her bed gloomy and disconsolate. Suddenly she burst out, 'No I am not a cad. Helen has come very near to persuading me that I am but I really am not. We both went into this with our eyes open, and Helen fully as deliberately as myself. I never intentionally made her suffer however much she may think I did. No if one goes in, one must be willing to stand for the whole game and take the full responsibility of their own share.' [*Q.E.D.*, 108]

One night Jeff Campbell was lying in his bed with his thinking, and night after night now he could not do any sleeping for his thinking. To-night suddenly he sat up in his bed, and it all came clear to him, and he pounded his pillow with his fist, and he almost shouted out alone there to him, 'I ain't a brute the way Melanctha has been saying. Its all wrong the way I been worried thinking. We did begin fair, each not for the other but for ourselves, what we were wanting. Melanctha Herbert did it just like I did it, because she liked it bad enough to want to stand it. It's all wrong in me to think it any way except the way we really did it.' ["Melanctha," 178]

The narrator in *Q.E.D.* is attempting to describe Adele's state of mind with words such as "gloomy," and "disconsolate." But after all, the description is external — perhaps because the phrase that follows it, "Suddenly she burst out," is unconvincing and overly violent, and therefore obtrusive. The narrator's voice in the second passage is much more convincing. Stein has made it more convincing by keeping the narrator's language in concert with Jeff's own. Her use of the gerunds "his thinking," and "any sleeping," echoes Jeff's use of the present participle in his thoughts. The narrator blends with Jeff again in the phrase, "and it all came clear to him." Strictly speaking, that phrase is not standard English; but it is the English that Jeff speaks, and so by using Jeff's speech patterns in the narration, Stein's narrator in "Melanctha" creates an "intense illusion of truth," as Booth terms this effect (45) — which the narrator of *Q.E.D.* fails to accomplish.

The use of the present participle reflects another important shift in Gertrude Stein's interests as a writer — her interest in what she termed "present immediacy."[27] In "Composition as Explanation"[28] she describes this interest at some length.

> In beginning writing I wrote a book called *Three Lives* this was written in 1905. I wrote a negro story called "Melanctha." In that there was a constant recurring and beginning there was a marked direction in the direction of being in the present although naturally I had been accustomed to past present and future, and why, because the composition forming around me was a prolonged present. A composition of a prolonged present is a natural composition in the world as it has been these thirty years it was more and more a prolonged present. I created then a prolonged present. . . . [517]

As we shall see later in this book, her interest in the complexities inherent in recreating "present immediacy" was life-long. She wrote:

> I was trying to get this present immediacy without trying to drag in anything else. I had to use present participles, new constructions of grammar. The grammar-constructions are correct, but they are changed, in order to get this immediacy. In short, from that time I have been trying in every possible way to get the sense of immediacy, and practically all the work I have done has been in that direction.[29]

We shall return to Stein's absorption in the problems of time again and again. But this was not the only narrative technique she brought to "Melanctha." Still another innovation is the device of narrative repetition (or "insistence" as Stein would term the device). It occurs in "The Good Anna," but in only one recurrent phrase, "Anna led an arduous and troubled life" (11, 13, 21). The device heavily permeates "Melanctha," and seems to have been invented by Gertrude Stein.[30]

Such narrative repetition occurs most obviously with Melanctha's mother. She enters the story with the following reference by the narrator:

> Melanctha Herbert had been raised to be religious, by her mother. Melanctha had not liked her mother very well. This mother, 'Mis' Herbert, as her neighbors called her, had been a sweet appearing and dignified and pleasant, pale yellow, colored woman. 'Mis' Herbert had always been a little wandering and mysterious and uncertain in her ways. [89-90]

A short while later, the narrator introduces Melanctha's father, and the mother is again mentioned.

> Melanctha's father was a big black virile negro. He only came once in a while to where Melanctha and her mother lived, but always that pleasant, sweet-appearing, pale yellow woman, mysterious and uncertain and wandering in her ways, was close in sympathy and thinking to her big black virile husband. [90]

And, a few pages later, " 'Mis' Herbert as her neighbors called her was never heard even to speak of her husband or her daughter. She was always pleasant, sweet-appearing, mysterious and uncertain, and a little wandering in her ways" (93).

The effects of the rhythmic insistence (as Stein would later term this technique) begin to show themselves a few pages later.

> Boys had never meant much to Melanctha. They had always been too young to content her. Melanctha had a strong respect for any kind of successful power. It was this that always kept

Melanctha nearer, in her feeling toward her virile and unendurable black father, than she ever was in her feeling for her pale yellow, sweet-appearing mother. The things she had in her of her mother, never made her feel respect. [96]

The cumulative effect of repeated phrases like "pale yellow," and "sweet-appearing," by the narrator is to make the mother starkly one-dimensional without seeming to do so. She becomes passive and ineffectual in the mind of a reader who is told over and over again that she is "pale yellow," and "sweet-appearing." And when we learn that her daughter had no respect for her, we believe it without further proof.

This is a very economical device of narration. The mother is never rendered in any scene in this story — in fact the mother never even speaks. Her usefulness to the story is as a contrast to the wildness and restlessness of her daughter. Because of this fact, it would have been artistically wasteful and unnecessary to have several scenes in which the mother is "shown" to be passive and ineffectual — especially when a few repetitions such as the ones quoted could be used so effectively and economically instead.

There are literally hundreds of examples of the use of repetition to be found throughout "Melanctha." Indeed, blended with the device of tuning the narrator's language to the rhythms and the patterns of the characters, it is the major technique used in "Melanctha."

Of course the device is not always used for the same effect. The narrator is not the only one who uses repetition effectively. There is a great deal of repetition in the dialogue as well. It is used in dialogue because Gertrude Stein believed that people talk that way. She believed that people reveal themselves through their slow, cumulative repetitions; therefore that was a valid way to reveal them in fiction. However, Gertrude Stein never referred to this device as repetition. In one of the lectures she gave during her triumphant return to America in 1935 she said, "Then also there is the important question of repetition and is there any such thing. Is there repetition or is there insistence. I am inclined to believe there is no such thing as repetition."[31]

She called it "insistence," or "emphasis," not repetition. Her distinction is made clearer in her own words:

> Think about all the detective stories everybody reads. The kind of crime is the same, and the idea of the story is very often the same, take for example a man like Wallace, he always has the same theme, take a man like Fletcher he always has the same theme, take any American ones, they too always have the scene, the same scene, the kind of invention that is necessary to make a general scheme is very limited in everybody's experience, every time one of the hundreds of times a newspaper man makes fun of my writing and of my repetition he always has the same theme, always having the same theme, that is, if you like, repetition, that is if you like the repeating that is the same thing, but once started expressing this thing, expressing any thing there can be no repetition because the essence of that expression is insistence, and if you insist you must each time use emphasis and if you use emphasis it is not possible while anybody is alive that they should use exactly the same emphasis. And so let us think seriously of the difference between repetition and insistence. [166-67]

As she very often did during these lectures, Gertrude Stein illustrated her thesis with some anecdote, either autobiographical or historical. In the case of the passage quoted above, she used a charming autobiographical event in elucidation:

> When I first realized the inevitable repetition in human ex-

pression that was not repetition but insistence . . . was when at about seventeen years of age, I left the more or less internal and solitary and concentrated life I led in California and came to Baltimore and lived with . . . principally with a whole group of very lively little aunts who had to know anything.

If they had to know anything and anybody does they naturally had to say and hear it often, anybody does, and as there were ten and eleven of them they did have to say and hear said whatever was said and any one not hearing what it was they said had to come in to hear what had been said. That inevitably made everything said often. I began then to consciously listen to what anybody was saying and what they did say while they were saying what they were saying. . . . No matter how often what happened had happened any time any one told anything there was no repetition. . . .

When all these eleven little aunts were listening as they were talking gradually some one of them was no longer listening. When this happened it might be that the time had come that any one or one of them was beginning repeating, that is was ceasing to be insisting. . . . [168-69]

Note the cumulative *insistence* of the word "certainly" in the following speech that Jeff Campbell makes to Melanctha:

Melanctha Herbert . . . I certainly after all this time I know you, I certainly do know little, real about you. You see, Melanctha, it's like this way with me; . . . You see it's just this way, with me now, Melanctha. Sometimes you seem like one kind of a girl to me, and sometimes you are like a girl that is all different to me, and the two kinds of girls is certainly very different to each other, and I can't see any way they seem to have much to do, to be together in you. They certainly don't seem to be made much like as if they could have anything really to do with each other. Sometimes you are a girl to me I certainly never would be trusting, . . . and yet all that I just been saying is certainly you one way I often see you. . . . And then certainly sometimes, Melanctha, you certainly is all a different creature, and sometimes then there comes out in you what is certainly a thing, like a real beauty. I certainly, Melanctha, never can tell just how it is that it comes so lovely. Seems to me when it comes it's got a real sweetness, that is more wonderful than a pure flower, and a gentleness, that is more tender than the sunshine, and a kindness, that makes one feel like summer . . . and it does certainly seem to be real for the little while it's lasting, . . . and it gives me to feel like I certainly had got real religion. And then when I got rich with such a feeling, comes all that other girl, and then that seems more likely that that is really you what's honest, and then I certainly do get awful afraid to come to you, and I certainly never do feel I could be very trusting with you. And then I certainly don't know anything at all about you, and I certainly don't know which is a real Melanctha Herbert, and I certainly don't feel no longer, I ever want to talk to you. Tell me honest, Melanctha, which is the way that is you really, when you are alone, and real, and all honest. Tell me, Melanctha, for I certainly do want to know it. [138-39]

When the reader recalls what Gertrude Stein said about her concern with capturing "present immediacy," the cumulative effects of this passage can readily be apprehended.[32] The frequent use of the word "certainly" not only adds to the credibility of Jeff as a "real" person speaking, but it forces the pace of his speech to become very slow and quiet, thereby allowing the weight and value of his thoughts to emerge — very slowly, but very surely. Then, of course, toward the end of the speech, as the use of "certainly" becomes even more frequent, the reverse effect, of increased pacing, emerges. The device culminates in the emergence of Jeff as an immediate *presence* which can be visualized in all its slow, rhythmic, quiet concern over his problems with Melanctha.

It is here, then, in the "Melanctha" story of *Three Lives* that Gertrude Stein appears to have made the greatest innovations of her early years. That she is still indebted to Flaubert is easily recognized in the description of Melanctha's death, which bears a close resemblance to the voice of the impassive narrator of the other two stories from *Three Lives:*

> Then Melanctha got very sick again, she began to cough and sweat and be so weak she could not stand to do her work.
>
> Melanctha went back to the hospital, and there the Doctor told her she had the consumption, and before long she would surely die. They sent her where she would be taken care of, a home for poor consumptives, and there Melanctha stayed until she died. [235-36]

But, Stein had also opened a new pathway for herself as can be seen in the new techniques for narration that she had invented.

"ADA"

The principal work of the period shortly after the writing of *Three Lives* was, of course, *The Making of Americans*, and after that the writing of portraits, of which "Ada"[33] was the first. Although there are some difficulties involved in dating Stein's writings exactly, because so many of her works were not published until years after they were written, some authoritative chronology is available. Robert B. Haas and Donald C. Gallup[34] worked on these matters with Gertrude Stein shortly before her death in 1946. Haas and Gallup place the writing of *The Making of Americans* between the years 1903 and 1908 — immediately after *Three Lives* (written in 1904 and 1905).[35]

Although *The Making of Americans* is an important work in the development of the artistry of Gertrude Stein, a full discussion of it is not necessary here since the narrative techniques employed in it are also amply in evidence in her shorter works (*The Making of Americans* is one-thousand pages long). No work on Gertrude Stein is complete, however, without some mention of this vast project.

The Making of Americans is, ostensibly, a history of two families — the Dehnings and the Herslands — who have emigrated from Germany to the United States. The book begins as if it were to have characters, a plot, and a narrator. But early in it the narrator altogether ceases to "tell a story," in the conventional sense, and the work becomes a complex mixture of several narrative techniques.

From Gertrude Stein's own statements one can see the rambling and unwieldy "thing" the book would turn out to be:

> *The Making of Americans* is a very important thing and everybody ought to be reading at it or it, and now I am trying to do it again to say everything about everything, only then I was wanting to write a history of every individual person who ever is or was or shall be living. . . .[36]

It can easily be seen from such a statement that a work written with an aim as ambitious as this would suffer greatly from what Wayne Booth terms a lack of "dramatic heightening,"[37] and focus. But, it must also be recognized that Gertrude Stein did not care about such considerations:

> After all, to me one human being is as important as another human being, and you might say that the landscape has the same values, a blade of grass has the same value as a tree. Because the realism of the people who did realism before was a realism of trying to make people real. I was not interested in making the people real but in the essence or, as a painter would call it, value. . . .

In *The Making of Americans* I began the same thing. In trying to make a history of the world my idea here was to write the life of every individual who could possibly live on the earth. I hoped to realize that ambition. My intention was to cover every possible variety of human type in it. . . . I wanted each one to have the same value. I was not at all interested in the little or big men but to realize absolutely every variety of human experience that it was possible to have, every type, every style and nuance. . . .[38]

Perhaps it can be foreseen that any novelist who attempts such a catalogue of human characteristics runs the risk of producing, not a novel, but a catalogue of human characteristics. And, to some extent, that is what happens in *The Making of Americans*. It must be kept in mind, however, that Gertrude Stein's interests did not lie in the same direction as the nineteenth-century "story" writers. In fact, by the final chapter of this novel there is no longer a plot (in the same sense as the plot that began the work); the original characters are no longer recognizable, and the narrator who is initially present has become a completely different entity. About this change in interest, Stein wrote:

When I was up against the difficulty of putting down the complete conception that I had of an individual, the complete rhythm of a personality that I had gradually acquired by listening seeing feeling and experience, I was faced by the trouble that I had acquired all this knowledge gradually but when I had it I had it completely at one time. Now that may never have been a trouble to you but it was a terrible trouble to me. And a great deal of The Making of Americans was a struggle to do this thing, to make a whole present of something that it had taken a great deal of time to find out, but it was a whole there then within me and as such it had to be said.

That then and ever since has been a great deal of my work and it is that which has made me try so many ways to tell my story.

In The Making of Americans I tried it in a variety of ways. And my sentences grew longer and longer, my imaginary dependent clauses were constantly being dropped out, I struggled with relations between they them and then, I began with a relation between tenses that sometimes almost seemed to do it. And I went on and on and then one day after I had written a thousand pages, this was in 1908 I just did not go on any more.[39]

The last chapter of *The Making of Americans* — with its almost exclusive use of indefinite pronouns as subjects of sentences — illustrates these important matters. That chapter begins:

> Any one has come to be a dead one. Any one has not come to be such a one to be a dead one. Many who are living have not come yet to be a dead one. Many who were living have come to be a dead one. Any one has come not to be a dead one. Any one has come to be a dead one.[40]

It is interesting to recall, while considering the above paragraph, the many interests that had come to absorb Stein by this point in her career: at least two of them are represented in this paragraph. She was struggling to capture an immediate presence, and she was trying to maintain what she saw as the equal value of all things. It is probably fair to say that after attempting one more longer work — *A Long Gay Book*[41] (which she soon abandoned for the same reasons that she simply stopped writing *The Making of Americans*)[42] — she turned to the more concentrated writing of portraits, in which she could explore her interests microscopically.

The first portrait Gertrude Stein wrote was "Ada."[43] It was a portrait of Alice B. Toklas, who had come to live with Leo and Gertrude Stein in Paris in 1907,[44] and is interesting for a variety of reasons.

It is one of the few (of the thirty-five or so to follow) that have a story line with a beginning, a middle, and an end. It is highly intelligible without needing either knowledge of the subject matter or extensive footnoting, and it is a fairly straightforward narrative told in accessible language. As we will see, this is one of the last times, for some years to come, that Gertrude Stein would write so intelligibly.

"Ada" is only about one-thousand words in length. Ostensibly it is a "chronology in the life of this girl Ada."[45] But, as can easily be imagined, any chronology of anyone's life done in one thousand words must be highly selective indeed, and, of course this one is. The "story" line is divided into two parts — that which happened to Ada before she actually enters the story; and that which happens to Ada after she has entered the story. This short piece is notable because it includes two entirely different kinds of narrative techniques to explicate the two parts of Ada's life.

The first part of the story (about the first third of the narrative) discusses Ada's father and brother, and is told by a third-person, objective narrator. The following are the first three paragraphs from "Ada," quoted in their entirety so that this narrator may be contrasted more effectively with the narrator of the remainder of the portrait.

> Barnes Colhard did not say he would not do it but he did not do it. He did it and then he did not do it, he did not ever think about it. He just thought some time he might do something.
>
> His father Mr. Abram Colhard spoke about it to every one and very many of them spoke to Barnes Colhard about it and he always listened to them.
>
> Then Barnes fell in love with a very nice girl and she would not marry him. He cried then, his father Mr. Abram Colhard comforted him and they took a trip and Barnes promised he would do what his father wanted him to be doing. He did not do the

thing, he thought he would do another thing, he did not do the other thing, his father Mr. Colhard did not want him to do the other thing. He really did not do anything then. When he was a good deal older he married a very rich girl. He had thought perhaps he would not propose to her but his sister wrote to him that it would be a good thing. He married the rich girl and she thought he was the most wonderful man and one who knew everything. Barnes never spent more than the income of the fortune he and his wife had then, that is to say they did not spend more than the income and this was a surprise to very many who knew about him and about his marrying the girl who had such a large fortune. He had a happy life while he was living and after he was dead his wife and children remembered him. [14]

We have seen Stein use this third-person, objective narrator in *Three Lives*. But, in that work, her principal narrative technique was the blending of the patterns and rhythms of the narrator's speech with those of the characters. In "Ada," on the other hand, there is no dialogue. Only the narrator "speaks." But it is easy to see from the passage quoted above that even though Barnes Colhard and his father are not given actual dialogue, the narrator has managed to communicate a great deal of their "sound" without ever allowing them to "sound," so to speak. Barnes Colhard is "rendered" in all of his dependence and indecisiveness without the narrator ever using those words to describe him. This is accomplished through the very language of the narration itself in such phrases as, "Barnes Colhard did not say he would not do it but he did not do it," and "He did it and then he did not do it. . . ." This is the same technique we saw in *Three Lives*, without the reinforcing dialogue.[46]

With the entrance of Ada into the story, however, the

narrative technique changes. The first change is in the kinds of factual data given about the character. When the narrator discusses the father or the brother, the information about them is limited to externals, to events. But as Ada enters the action, we see an immediate change. Although Ada is not mentioned by name until later in the portrait, the following quotation introduces her:

> He had a sister who also was successful enough in being one being living. His sister was one who came to be happier than most people come to be in living. She came to be a completely happy one. . . . [14]

We have seen previously Stein's use of the present participle in "Melanctha," but its use in "Ada" is quite different. In "Melanctha" it was used by the narrator to lend a sense of present immediacy to the time elements in the story, and to blend the speech patterns of Jeff Campbell with the narrative voice itself. In "Ada," because there is no dialogue, the use of the participle is different and deserves some explication.

This form as a narrative device not directly concerned with the fiber of the story (as it was in "Melanctha") first appeared in *The Making of Americans.* The last chapter of that book has no characters other than those suggested by indefinite pronouns. The implication is that the narrator of that section is no longer interested in either the plot previously established, or in any specific character. In fact, the last chapter is concerned, apparently, with an investigation into such considerations as "knowing," "understanding," and "being one being living." Examples, such as this brief one, could be taken at random from any page of the last chapter:

Some are certain that any one is one being living. Some are knowing only this thing about everything, that any one is one being living. Some are knowing that not any one is one being living. Some are knowing that any one who is one being living is one knowing something of this thing. Some are ones not understanding anything of any such thing, of any one knowing something of this thing that any one is being one being living. [396]

To the reader who has been led for several hundreds of pages by the Aristotelian expectation that the final chapter of *The Making of Americans* will conclude the history of the families it has been dealing with, this final chapter is, to say the least, confusing.[47] But that is just the point, for Stein had become interested in something other than conventional (Aristotelian) considerations in the novel. It is essential to understand what she was doing here before we return to "Ada," because it is in "Ada" that she begins a long process — repeated in all her remaining work, as well as in the rest of her portraits — of employing this participle form in an attempt to capture the "inner reality"[48] of subject matter which she considered to be changing constantly even while she was attempting to capture it.

Gertrude Stein expressed this concern in these words:

. . . the making of a portrait of any one is as they are existing and as they are existing has nothing to do with remembering any one or anything. . . .

Funnily enough the cinema has offered a solution of this thing. By a continuously moving picture of any one there is no memory of any other thing and there is that thing existing, it is in a way if you like one portrait of anything not a number of them.

. . . in *The Making of Americans*, I was doing what the cinema

was doing, I was making a continuous succession of the statement of what that person was until I had not many things but
one thing.[49]

The narrator, then, is no longer attempting to tell a
story in the Aristotelian sense. He is attempting to present an immediate, continuous progression of states.
Stein continues:

> In a cinema picture no two pictures are exactly alike each one is
> just that much different from the one before, and so in those
> early portraits there was ... as there was in *The Making of
> Americans* no repetition. Each time that I said the somebody
> whose portrait I was writing was something that something
> was just that much different from what I had just said that
> somebody was and little by little in this way a whole portrait
> came into being .... [177]

"Ada" is a very much shortened form of a work in
which a narrator begins by telling a story in a factual
and impassive manner, then, much as in *The Making of
Americans,* suddenly shifts to a cinema-like compilation
of frame upon frame — each one slightly different from
the rest — in an effort to capture the immediacy of the
subject.

After Ada is introduced as a character, the narrator
tells us a bit about her relationship with her mother,
whom she loves. After the mother dies, the narrator
tells us,

> The daughter then kept house for her father and took care of her
> brother. There were many relations who lived with them. The
> daughter did not like them to live with them and she did not
> like them to die with them. .... She told her father Mr. Abram
> Colhard that she did not like it at all being one being living
> then. [15]

The remainder of "Ada" is then devoted to her leaving

her father and going to another country to live. It is at this point, when Ada reaches her new country, that we see the cinema technique come to full fruition in the narration:

> She came to be happier than anybody else who was living then. It is easy to believe this thing. She was telling some one, who was loving every story that was charming. Some one who was living was almost always listening. Some one who was loving was almost always listening. That one who was loving was almost always listening. That one who was loving was telling about being one then listening. That one being loving was then telling stories having a beginning and a middle and an ending. That one was then one always completely listening. Ada was then one and all her living then one completely telling stories that were charming, completely listening to stories having a beginning and a middle and an ending. Trembling was all living, living was all loving, some one was then the other one. Certainly this one was loving this Ada then. And certainly Ada all her living then was happier in living than any one else who ever could, who was, who is, who ever will be living. [16]

It is probably true, as Bridgman points out, that "Ada" is a "love poem,"[50] but that does not account fully for the flight of lyricism at the end of this portrait. Flights of this nature were to become almost formulaic at the ends of Stein's portraits — whether or not any particular portrait was on the subject, or about an object, of love. The investigation of three more portraits from this period will serve to strengthen this point.

Before turning to the other portraits, it would be useful here to summarize a few conclusions about "Ada." The narrator we have seen at the beginning of "Ada" does not recur for many years in Stein's work. As her considerations and interests began to change, she found the impassive, factual narrator used so effectively in early pieces, and then again at the beginning of "Ada," an ineffectual device when her interests left off telling a clearly defined story and turned to a concern with a different kind of reality. The narrative technique needed to express efficiently, "He had a happy life while he was living and after he was dead his wife and children remembered him," is, after all, quite different from the one needed for, "trembling is all living." Because the needs are different, the narrator switches from one technique to another as those needs shift in "Ada."

"TWO: GERTRUDE STEIN AND HER BROTHER"

In *The Making of Americans*, the narrator says, three times, "I write for myself and strangers" (211, 282). Gertrude Stein repudiated this as a philosophical concept of writing in a lecture at Oxford in 1936 with the words:

> I once wrote in *The Making of Americans* I write for myself and strangers but that was merely a literary formalising for if I did write for myself and strangers if I did I would not really be writing because already then identity would take the place of entity.[51]

Yet in the following year (1937), she wrote again as if she *had* written for strangers:

> ... Picasso used to be fond of saying that when everybody knew about you and admired your work there were just about the same two or three who were really interested as when nobody knew about you, but does it make any difference. In writing the Making of Americans I said I write for myself and strangers and then later now I know these strangers, are they still strangers, ...[52]

The importance of this point can be seen easily by anyone who reads the long portrait "Two: Gertrude Stein and Her Brother"[53] *without* some previous knowledge of the life and relationship of Gertrude Stein and her brother Leo. Unlike "Ada," the "story" is simply not comprehensible without prior biographical information. So, either Gertrude Stein was writing it for herself, or for people who already knew the facts of the relationship. The work was not published until after her death,[54] which makes it likely that she was, after all, writing it for herself.[55]

Some biographical material must be supplied before this "portrait" can be discussed. Gertrude Stein and her brother Leo were given a piece of bizarre information when they were children. Their parents had made an agreement when they married to have five children. The parents had the five and stopped. Gertrude and Leo were not among those five children. However, two of the original five died in infancy and the parents replaced them with Leo, then Gertrude. In *Everybody's Autobiography*, Gertrude Stein comments on these bizarre circumstances:

> Then there was the fear of dying, anything living knows about that, and when that happens anybody can think if I had died before there was anything but there is no thinking that one was never born until you hear accidently that there were to be five children and if two little ones had not died there would be no Gertrude Stein, of course not.
>
> Identity always worries me and memory and eternity. [115]

Gertrude and Leo Stein were two years apart in age, and were inseparable companions in their childhood.[56] When they grew up and Leo went off to Harvard, Gertrude followed him to the Harvard Annex (now

Radcliffe). When Leo went to visit in Europe, Gertrude often travelled with him. And, when Leo moved permanently to Europe, Gertrude followed him there, too, and shared an apartment with him until 1914.[57]

Apparently the relationship was one of a younger sister's adoration of her brother. At college she even wrote a theme on the subject.[58] By the time she joined Leo in Paris, in 1903, to remain permanently abroad, she had been graduated from college and had spent four years at the Johns Hopkins Medical School working toward a medical degree. She was twenty-nine years old at the time she moved in with her brother, and there was certain to be a change in the youthful adoration pattern.

Moreover, Leo Stein apparently had some personal problems. Although the Stein children had some private income (thanks to their father's inheritance, which the older brother, Mike, invested wisely for all the children), neither Leo nor Gertrude Stein's goal-oriented ethics would allow them simply to do nothing with their lives. Leo was especially nervous about his lack of concrete accomplishment and went from painting to writing, and finally became an art critic, in an agonizing series of efforts to prove the brilliance he was convinced he possessed.[59]

It was during this period that Gertrude Stein began to write in earnest. John Brinnin states:

> Gertrude was now spending long hours at her desk every night — a practice to which Leo gave but passing attention, since his interests were centered exclusively in himself and the fabulous ideas that elated him one day and wracked him the next. Interminably fingering his neuroses, he continued to make cantankerous assays into the field of aesthetics, now and then actually tried to paint. . . . [79]

Gertrude and Leo Stein gave small dinner parties, with many guests dropping in afterward, every Saturday night. At these Leo Stein would "hold court" for many hours, indulging himself at length in a monologue on any subject of interest to him. Gertrude wrote:

> We were settled in Paris together and we were always together and I was writing. Everybody began to come in and my brother was talking, and this is what is interesting, what makes one of the things that used to make me say something. I did not care for any one being intelligent because if they are intelligent they talk as if they were preparing to change something.[60]

She summarizes the beginning of the end of their relationship by saying, "Well any way, he continued to believe in what he was saying when he was arguing and I began not to find it interesting.[61]

It was Leo's reaction to his sister's writings which brought about the final break between them. Gertrude Stein was writing *The Making of Americans* at the time. She writes,

> I was writing in the way I was writing. I did not show what I was doing to my brother, he looked at it and he did not say anything. Why not. Well there was nothing to say about it and really I had nothing to say about it. Gradually he had something to say about it. I did not hear him say it. Slowly we were not saying anything about it that is we never had said anything about it.[62]

Leo Stein obviously never took his younger sister seriously as an artist. She continues,

> Slowly and in a way it was not astonishing but slowly I was knowing that I was a genius and it was happening and I did not say anything but I was almost ready to begin to say something. My brother began saying something and this is what he said.

He said it was not it it was I. If I was not there to be there with what I did then what I did would not be what it was. In other words if no one knew me actually then the things I did would not be what they were.[63]

Gertrude Stein is having her little joke in the above passage — a joke we will discuss later in connection with the narrator in *Everybody's Autobiography*. By refusing to punctuate so that the reader can distinguish between Leo's and Gertrude's remarks, Stein has made the passage more difficult to read than it would be otherwise. What she is saying, of course, is that Leo told her she was not a genius; that everything she had ever done, or ever would do, she owed directly to his influence and tutelage; and, that if he had not been around, she would never have produced anything on her own.

She continues:

He did not say it to me but he said it so that it would be true for me. And it did not trouble me and as it did not trouble me I knew it was not true and a little as it did not trouble me he knew it was not true.

But it destroyed him for me and it destroyed me for him. . . . The only thing about it was that it was I who was the genius, there was no reason for it but I was, and he was not there was a reason for it but he was not and that was the beginning of the ending and we always had been together and now we were never at all together. Little by little we never met again. [77]

With this background in mind, we can proceed to the discussion of the narrative techniques Gertrude Stein used to tell the story of this relationship in the long portrait, "Two: Gertrude Stein and Her Brother," written between 1910 and 1912.[64]

This portrait employs some of the narrative techniques Gertrude Stein had used before, but adds a new element in the narrator which is akin to the Greek *histor*.[65]

Stein's careful manipulation of language — especially the participle — to simulate rhythms of speech-and-time flow has been demonstrated in the discussion of *Three Lives*. In "Two," participial forms are used to the outer reaches of possibility — there is hardly an instance of simple verb forms in the whole one-hundred-forty-one-page portrait. Furthermore, there is no dialogue in this portrait — it consists entirely of description by the narrator. Therefore, as in "Ada," the manipulation of language in this portrait is not meant to correspond directly to speech patterns. The following example is the opening paragraph of "Two: Gertrude Stein and Her Brother."

> The sound there is in them comes out from them. Each one of them has sound in them. Each one of them has sound coming out of them. There are two of them. One of them is a man and one of them is a woman. They are both living. They are both ones that quite enough are knowing. Quite enough are knowing each one of them. Sound is coming out of each one of them, out of each one of the two of them. Sound is in them in each one of the two of them. Each one of the two of them is having sound coming out of them. [1]

The use of the participial forms here is close in nature to that in "Ada." The narrator is again utilizing the cinema-like technique Stein termed "insistence," or "emphasis," rather than repetition. The narrator is clearly compiling sentences which differ only slightly from the others in the same paragraph, as was the case at the end of "Ada."

But, the key difference between "Ada" and this

portrait lies in the function of the narrator.

In "Ada," the narrator of the second part of the portrait, while still a third-person narrator, has left the distance he had maintained in the first part to become a singer, or lyricist. It was suggested during the discussion of "Ada" that a phrase such as "trembling was all living," is not the language of the impassive narrator but, rather, the language of a narrator inside the consciousness of the character being described.

While the narrator of "Two" is also inside the characters being described (Stein uses the third person in this portrait also), he is neither the impassive narrator of Stein's early works, nor the lyricist of "Ada." The difference is that the narrator of "Two" appears to be attempting, slowly and laboriously, to examine the inner realities of the characters for the purpose of reaching the truths about their relationships. The narrators of Stein's previous works knew these truths from the beginning.

Consider the following example from "Two." (Proper names are never used in this work.)

> She was thinking in being one who was a different one in being one than he was in being one. Sound was coming out of her and she was knowing this thing. Sound had been coming out of him and she had been knowing this thing. She was thinking in being a different one than he was in having sound come out of her than came out of him. . . . She had sound coming out of her. She was knowing that thing. She had had sound coming out of her, she was knowing that thing. He had had sound coming out of him, she was knowing that thing. He had sound coming out of him, she was knowing this thing. . . . She was different in being one being one. She was knowing that thing. [5-6]

The narrator continues to investigate the relationship between these two characters in the language of "sound sounding out of them" for a little more than half of this portrait — for in fact, the first eighty-seven pages. Clearly, the narrator had already made the point that the man was a pompous windbag who never gave the woman a chance to find her own identity much earlier than eight-seven pages would require, but the narrator is not interested in merely making the point. The narrator is most anxious to present and to examine all the nuances of the evidence. Such is the province of the *histor* as narrator.

The term *histor* is used and defined by Robert Scholes and Robert Kellogg in their book, *The Nature of Narrative*,[66] as follows:

> The Greek historians in their narratives substitute for the authority of tradition a new kind of authority. The *histor* as narrator is not a recorder or recounter but an investigator. He examines the past with an eye toward separating out actuality from myth. Herodotus takes his authority not so much from his sources as from the critical spirit with which he means to approach those sources. Where the traditional poet must confine himself to one version of his story, the *histor* can present conflicting versions in his search for the truth of fact. Thucydides is the perfect type of the ancient *histor,* basing his authority on the accuracy of conclusions he has drawn from evidence he has gathered. [242-43]

There is no intention, of course, of suggesting that the similarities between Stein's narrator here and the *histor* of Greek tradition are anything more than conceptual. But the term is a useful one for describing a narrator who requires eighty-seven pages to say that sound is sounding out of two characters. Surely this is an amassing of evidence on which to base whatever conclusions he will eventually draw. Such is the concept of the *histor* as narrator.

The remainder of the portrait contains two further biographical considerations in the lives of the two characters. The first one is that the woman's work is becoming increasingly important to her:

> If he says that any one saying that the thing that has happened means something is mistaken he says that the one saying what that one is saying is showing that that one is not grasping what that one cannot grasp. He himself and he is one thinking, he himself and he is one repeating, he himself and he is one predicting, he himself and he is one understanding, he himself and he is one reasoning, he himself and only what he has said is what he can say, he himself and he is completing explaining, he himself and all he is arranging, he himself and he is demonstrating . . . . [95]

The second biographical consideration is the entrance of Alice B. Toklas into the lives of the two characters, followed by the final break between the brother and sister.[67] (The two "she's" in the following section appear to be Gertrude Stein and Alice Toklas.)[68]

> She and if she was one she was not one and there were two, she and she was there and she had the same time as all there is of any of all that which as change has enough of all there is of any expressing, she and if she is all there will be is what there is if she is all of what there will be. She was encouraged and the tune which was that element is the one that if she is there to be included is the one to say that which if it the one is that one and there has been all of that said. [135-36]

It can be seen from this passage that the narrator, although still the third-person *histor*, has shifted tactics somewhat. He is not stringing together one participle after another. He is no longer amassing thousands of variations on the one theme of sound sounding out of a man and a woman: "She and if she was one she was not one and there were two." Not only do we see that another character has entered the story, but we also see the narrator's interest shift from the relationship between the man and woman — which the narrator sees as crippling to the woman — to a newfound sense of identity for that woman. "She was encouraged . . . ." The woman has "surfaced" so to speak, through not being one, but now being two. The important element in the biographical consideration at this point is that the narrator has changed his method in this section.[69]

Whereas the method of the first section relied heavily on the sentence after sentence compilation of slightly differing content, the method of the above passage, and of the rest of the portrait, is the shift away from representational language to language that is an autotelic entity. Consider the very last sentences of the portrait, "A belief that has translation is not all there is of exaltation. He had all of any of that use" (142). Obviously the narrator of that sentence has not offered that as a logical, rational idea, although many of Stein's critics have attacked her nonrepresentational prose for not being representational. What is clear here is that by the end of this portrait Gertrude Stein had begun experimenting with language *for its own sake.* In Stein's own words:

> On the *Making of Americans* I had written about one thousand pages, and I finished the thing with a sort of rhapsody at the end. Then I started in to write *Matisse, Picasso, and Gertrude Stein.* You will see in each one of these stories that they began in the character of *Making of Americans,* and then in about the middle of it words began to be for the first time more important than the sentence structure or the paragraphs. Something happened. I mean I felt a need. I had thought this thing out and felt a need of breaking it down and forcing it into little pieces. I felt that I had lost contact with the words in building up these

Beethovian passages. I had lost that idea gained in my youth from the Seventeenth Century writers, and the little rhymes that used to run through my head from Shakespeare . . . got lost from the overall pattern.[70]

The experimentation is only in embryonic form in "Two," and comes to full fruition later, in her middle period. But an element of it runs through her next two early portraits, soon to be discussed. First, a brief review of what has been noted in "Two" may be useful.

"Two" is an autobiographical work told by a third-person narrator. The third-person narrator offered Stein the opportunity to examine central characters from what appeared to be a more objective stance than the first person would have allowed her. And, because she seemed to want to examine both her brother's and her own view of the relationship, the use of the third-person narrator allowed her greater distance than the first person would have. However, by the time the relationship between the brother and sister has been examined — and the breakdown justified — the narrator, no longer concerned with the relationship between them, switches from the language of the first section, to a more experimental form in the last. Gertrude Stein's language will fluctuate between the representational and the autotelic through the next two portraits before settling, in her middle period, to an almost total use of the nonrepresentational.

"THE PORTRAIT OF CONSTANCE FLETCHER"

"The Portrait of Constance Fletcher"[71] is one of the twenty-five portraits Gertrude Stein wrote between the years 1908 and 1912. Unlike either "Ada," or "Two," this portrait carries no story line at all. And, like "Two," this portrait cannot be understood without some previous knowledge of its ostensible subject, Constance Fletcher. (The term "ostensible" is used in this connection because only the first part of this portrait appears to have any recognizable subject.)

"The Portrait of Constance Fletcher" combines two narrative techniques already discussed: the *histor* who compiles evidence in a series of sentences relying heavily on the use of slightly shifting participles, and the narrator who quite suddenly shifts his language to the nonrepresentational. But, since the material included in this portrait is not autobiographical, the narrator is used in a manner different from that in either "Two," or "Ada."

Constance Fletcher was a novelist who, under the pseudonym George Fleming, wrote *Kismet.*[72] She was a close friend of Alice Toklas and Gertrude Stein, and apparently Stein was moved by some early events in Fletcher's life. This portrait (or the part in which Fletcher's life is obviously the subject) deals with only those early events. Rosalind Miller summarizes them:

> . . . as a child Constance Fletcher's mother fell in love with her son's tutor. The young Constance, although very upset, finally accompanied her mother and her stepfather to Italy. This break in the family probably caused the impressionable young girl to become more conscious of family relationships.[73]

Indeed, the opening paragraph of this portrait appears to refer to those events in Constance Fletcher's life.

> When she was quite a young one she knew she had been in a family living and that that family living was one that any one could be one not have been having if they were to be one being one not thinking about being one having been having family

living. She was one then when she was a young one thinking about having, about having been having family living. She was one thinking about this thinking, she was one feeling thinking about this thing, she was one feeling being one who could completely have feeling in thinking about being one who had had, who was having family living. [157]

The narrator then continues for another five hundred words or so (the portrait is some three thousand words long), attempting to describe the "inside" of his subject. (As Stein wrote about her concern in portraits, "If they are themselves inside them what are they and what has it to do with what they do.")[74]

It can be seen from the passage quoted that the narrator is again the *histor*, compiling cinema-like participial forms as evidence of some truth about the subject. This is a familiar technique by now, but it is not just a repetition of that technique. It will be noted that the passage contains several referents utilizing pronouns — both definite and indefinite — but no proper names. We have seen Stein do this before. But in this portrait, because the initial referent of the pronouns — Constance Fletcher — disappears shortly after being introduced, further use of the pronouns by the narrator bears discussion.

The name of anything is a metaphor which bears little relation to the object named. In our discussion of *Tender Buttons* we will see Stein consciously attempting to describe an object in its quiddity without ever referring to its name. Essentially the use of pronouns is an attempt to strike immediately "inside" a character by banishing that most external (and irrelevant) association — the character's name. The very first sentence of this portrait contains several examples of the use of the pronoun — not as a substitute for the proper noun — but as the nearest referent to the substantive without direct reference to its given name.[75] The point is that proper nouns (or indeed all nouns) are irrelevant, if one is considering something below surface reality.[76]

Constance Fletcher seems to disappear from this portrait in a sudden and dramatic shift by the narrator away from the definite pronoun "she" to a language which suddenly becomes self-generative. Note the shift in narrative technique in the following excerpt:

> . . . She was completely filling in to be a full one and she always was a full one. She was thinking in being a full one. She was feeling in being a full one. She was thinking in feeling in being a full one. She was feeling in thinking in being a full one.
>
> If they move in the shoe there is everything to do. They do not move in the shoe.
>
> The language of education is not replacing the special position that is the expression of the emanation of evil. There is an expression when contemplation is not connecting the object that is in position with the forehead that is returning looking. It is not overpowering. That is a cruel description. The memory is the same and surely the one who is not older is not dead yet although if he has been blind he is seeing. This has not any meaning. [159]

The narrator clearly has gone from a consideration of Constance Fletcher in the first paragraph to a demonstration of the special powers of words themselves — unrelated to any visible subject — in the second and third. In a sense, the narrator has become the only character in the story.

Just as suddenly as the first shift was made, another follows in the very next paragraph, which begins, "Oh the bells that are the same are not stirring and the languid grace is not out of place and the older fur is disappearing. There is not such an end" (159).

I mentioned earlier that a narrator who becomes a kind of rhapsodist at the end of each portrait would become an almost formulaic device in Stein's portraits. Indeed, in the portraits written between 1908 and 1912, the narrator is often the third-person *histor* at the beginning, and then a rhapsodist who, having dropped the original subject of the piece, now begins examining, or creating, a reality of his own.[77] Perhaps it is true, as Bridgman has said: "The idea had entered her mind that lyricism contained a fuller measure of truth than could ever be encircled by making endless, laboriously deliberate statements."[78] But there is more to it than that. Gertrude Stein was making the discovery that words have more dimensions than the merely representational. That words also have "play . . . of sight, sense and sound," as William Carlos Williams said of Stein's experiments,[79] was another dimension of her discovery during these early portraits.

"PORTRAIT OF MABEL DODGE AT THE VILLA CURONIA"

The choice of the "Portrait of Mabel Dodge at the Villa Curonia"[80] as the final selection from Gertrude Stein's early years was made because it is a transitional work. Unlike the previous portraits, this one contains neither a story line nor any characters. In place of these elements we have a narrator who appears to be struggling to wrest an objective reality from even the hands of the author.[81]

Mabel Dodge is nowhere in this portrait. At least there is no recognizable reference to her. And no background information on Mabel Dodge's life will clarify the reading of her portrait. It begins with what appears to be a reference to the Villa Curonia, but from that point on the language of the portrait becomes non-representational. The following is the opening of the portrait:

> The days are wonderful and the nights are wonderful and the life is pleasant.
>
> Bargaining is something and there is not that success. The intention is what if application has that accident results are re-appearing. They did not darken. That was not an adulteration.
>
> So much breathing has not the same place when there is that much beginning. So much breathing has not the same place when the ending is lessening. So much breathing has the same place and there must not be so much suggestion. There can be there the habit that there is if there is no need of resting. The absence is not alternative. [98]

This narrator is not compiling evidence in the way that Stein's *histor* narrators did, nor is this narrator ever talking about any people. The entire portrait is done with nouns as subjects of sentences, or, in some cases with the use of the beginning phrase, "There was . . . ," for example, "There was not that velvet spread when there was a pleasant head. The color was paler. The moving regulating is not a distinction. The place is there" (101).

Nevertheless, the narrator *is* compiling. But, in the case of this portrait, the narrator is compiling efforts at the recreation of individual words,[82] and not efforts at representational use of them. This is, in fact, what makes this portrait transitional. Most of Stein's earlier writings, though showing some kind of embryonic experimentation, were accessible, even if, occasionally, some background material needed to be supplied for the reader. But with the writing of "Mabel Dodge," Stein turned to a concern with the realities that language itself possesses, and she becomes, colloquially speaking, less intelligible.

This latter statement is an important idea, but in order to do full justice to it, we must now turn to a brief discussion of the intellectual and artistic atmosphere of Paris at the turn of the century. It is in this milieu that this unique experiment became one of Stein's principal concerns — it came to fruition in the middle years of her writing career.

NOTES

1 For a discussion of Stein's habit of writing in undated notebooks, see Michael J. Hoffman, *The Development of Abstractionism in the Writings of Gertrude Stein* (Philadelphia: University of Pennsylvania Press, 1965), pp. 102-03.

2 Gertrude Stein, "Quod Erat Demonstrandum," in *Fernhurst, Q.E.D., and Other Early Writings* [by] GERTRUDE STEIN, ed. Leon Katz (New York: Liveright, 1971).

3 Leon Katz, "Introduction," in *Fernhurst, Q.E.D., and Other Early Writings* [by] GERTRUDE STEIN, ed. Leon Katz (New York: Liveright, 1971), p. xv.

4 Donald Gallup, "A Note on the Texts," in *Fernhurst, Q.E.D., and Other Early Writings* [by] GERTRUDE STEIN, ed. Leon Katz (New York: Liveright, 1971).

5 Gertrude Stein, *Things As They Are* (Vermont: Pawlet Press, 1950).

6 Gertrude Stein, *The Autobiography of Alice B. Toklas* (New York: Harcourt, Brace, 1933), p. 104.

7 Hoffman, *The Development of Abstractionism*, p. 32, and Gallup, "A Note on the Texts."

8 See Wayne Booth, "The Confusion of Distance," *The Rhetoric of*

Fiction (Chicago: University of Chicago Press, 1966), pp. 311-36.

9 Alice Toklas's own words, written in 1963, seventeen years after the death of Gertrude Stein, render the quality of the relationship between the two women better than those of any outsiders writing about it. In *What is Remembered* (New York: Rinehart and Winston, 1963), p. 23, Alice Toklas, writing about her first meeting with Gertrude Stein (in 1907), says:

> In the room were Mr. and Mrs. (Mike) Stein and Gertrude Stein. It was Gertrude Stein who held my complete attention, as she did for all the many years I knew her until her death and all these empty ones since then.

10 I am not the only investigator to have seen these parallels. See Katz, "Introduction," p. viii, and Richard Bridgman, "Melanctha," *American Literature* 33 (November 1961), 350-59.

11 Henry James, *The Wings of the Dove* (New York: Modern Library, 1937), p. 82.

12 Perhaps the example given is enough to demonstrate that Gertrude Stein had read at least *The Wings of the Dove*. But, lest it be said that this one example represents evidence too slight, two other parallels between *Q.E.D.* and the James work are given. We have already seen Adele, in *Q.E.D.*, lamenting the fact that Helen cannot see "things as they are." Compare this with a summary of a conversation between Kate Croy and Milly Theale in *Wings of the Dove*:

> She gave away publicly, in this process, Lancaster Gate and everything it contained; she gave away, hand over hand, Milly's thrill continued to note, Aunt Maud and Aunt Maud's glories and Aunt Maud's complacencies; she gave herself away most of all, and it was naturally what most contributed to her candour. She didn't speak to her friend once more, in Aunt Maud's strain, of how they could scale the skies; she spoke, by her bright, perverse preference on this occasion, of the need, in the first place, of being neither stupid nor vulgar. It might have been a lesson, for our young American, in the art of seeing things as they were. . . . [Part I, p. 303]

Another parallel between the works is a comparison between

Kate Croy and Helen Thomas. Both women rely heavily on wealth as a value system, and both are referred to as "handsome English girls."

13 Hoffman, *The Development of Abstractionism*, p. 32.

14 Katz, "Introduction," p. xii.

15 *Ibid.*, p. vii.

16 I am indebted to Percy Lubbock, *The Craft of Fiction* (New York: Peter Smith, 1947) for my analysis of this method.

17 Gertrude Stein, *Three Lives* (New York: Modern Library, 1933). This work was first published (at Stein's expense) by the Grafton Press in 1909.

18 Gertrude Stein, "A Transatlantic Interview," in *Gertrude Stein, A Primer for the Gradual Understanding of Gertrude Stein*, ed. Robert Bartlett Haas (Los Angeles: Black Sparrow Press, 1971), p. 15.

19 Gustave Flaubert, "A Simple Soul," *The Works of Gustave Flaubert* (New York: Walter J. Black, 1904), p. 317.

20 Edmund Wilson, *Axel's Castle* (New York: Charles Scribner's Sons, 1945), p. 7.

21 Wayne Booth, *The Rhetoric of Fiction* (Chicago: University of Chicago Press, 1961), p. 68.

22 Which appear in Leon Katz, ed., *Fernhurst, Q.E.D., and Other Early Writings* [by] GERTRUDE STEIN (New York: Liveright, 1971).

23 It is always disconcerting to discover that other investigators have reached opposite conclusions. Richard Bridgman writes, "Other than giving *Three Lives* its original impetus, Flaubert was of minimal significance for Gertrude Stein." (Richard Bridgman, *Gertrude Stein in Pieces* [New York: Oxford University Press, 1970], p. 47.) I can only hope my discussion has proved otherwise.

24 Wilson, *Axel's Castle*, pp. 237-56.

25 Except for the major characters, who are reworkings of the white characters from *Q.E.D.*, the Blacks in "Melanctha" are quite

stereotyped. I agree with Bridgman, "Melanctha," *American Literature* 33 (November 1961):

> The race references in 'Melanctha' are infrequent, and when they do appear, they are stereotyped. Negroes possess shiny or greasy black faces; their eyeballs roll; their mouths gape open as they howl with laughter; they fight with razors, yell savagely, are often lazy, and are insistently virile. [P. 352]

26 To mention just a few of these critics, Carl Van Vechten, "Introduction," *Three Lives* (New York: Modern Library, 1933), p. x, says, "It is perhaps the first American story in which the Negro is regarded as a human being and not as an object for condescending compassion or derision."

Another statement is from Elizabeth Sprigge, *Gertrude Stein Her Life and Work* (London: Hamish Hamilton, 1957), p. 15, "As a medical student Gertrude Stein's work was very varied — she made a study of brain tracts and she assisted in the delivery of infants, particularly in the Negro quarter, which gave her fine material for her early story, 'Melanctha.' "

It is also tempting to quote Alice Toklas in her own autobiography, *What is Remembered,* p. 125. She refers to it also as a "fine story about Negroes."

27 Gertrude Stein, "How Writing is Written," *How Writing is Written,* Robert Bartlett Haas, ed. (Los Angeles: Black Sparrow Press, 1974), p. 155.

28 Gertrude Stein, "Composition as Explanation," *Selected Writings of Gertrude Stein,* Carl Van Vechten, ed. (New York: Vintage Books, 1972).

29 Gertrude Stein, "How Writing is Written," pp. 155-56.

30 See Wilson, *Axel's Castle,* p. 239.

31 Gertrude Stein, "Portraits and Repetitions," *Lectures in America* (New York: Random House, 1935), p. 166.

32 Of course, it must be acknowledged that to readers judging this technique by nineteenth-century story-telling standards such repetitions as these seem unmerited and boring. Certainly many of Stein's critics have made that very judgment — especially her early ones.

33 Gertrude Stein, "Ada," *Geography and Plays* (Boston: Four Seas, 1922), pp. 14-15.

34 Robert Bartlett Haas and Donald Clifford Gallup, *A Catalogue of the Published and Unpublished Writings of Gertrude Stein* (New Haven: Yale University Press, 1941).

35 *Ibid.*, p. 45.

36 Gertrude Stein, *Everybody's Autobiography* (New York: Random House, 1937), p. 99.

37 Booth, *The Rhetoric of Fiction*, p. 196.

38 Stein, "A Transatlantic Interview," p. 16.

39 Stein, "The Gradual Making of *The Making of Americans*," *Lectures in America* (New York: Random House, 1935), pp. 147-48.

40 Gertrude Stein, *The Making of Americans* (New York: Harcourt Brace, 1934), p. 395.

41 Stein, "The Gradual Making of *The Making of Americans*," p. 148.

42 *Ibid.*, p. 148.

43 Scholars differ on exactly when "Ada" was written. However, Janet Flanner, "Frame for Some Portraits," *Two and Other Early Portraits* (New Haven: Yale University Press, 1951), p. x, places it during the winter of 1908-1909, and notes,

> It was her first. That it was listed as No. 13 among the twenty-five portraits of this period has nothing to do with the fact, she said, that it was her first. She wrote it on a little block note pad and hurried with it into the kitchen in the apartment in the rue de Fleurus where her friend was cooking an excellent dinner and said in a high spirit of excitement and pleasure, 'You'll have to take whatever you're cooking off the stove so it won't burn or stop cooking it entirely for you must read this.'

44 Stein, *The Autobiography of Alice B. Toklas*, p. 4, 7.

45 Flanner, "Frame for Some Portraits," p. x.

69

46 In fact, there is a close resemblance between Barnes Colhard and Herman Kreder in "The Gentle Lena." Both are very passive characters dominated by fathers. In "The Gentle Lena," Herman is pressured by his father into marrying Lena.

47 Edmund Wilson found it unreadable. Wilson, *Axel's Castle*, p. 239.

48 This is a recurrent term used by Gertrude Stein. It is discussed in greater detail later as the term becomes more important to her work.

49 Stein, "Portraits and Repetitions," pp. 175-77.

50 Bridgman, *Gertrude Stein in Pieces*, p. 94.

51 Gertrude Stein, "What Are Masterpieces," in *Gertrude Stein: Writings and Lectures 1911-1945*, ed. Patricia Meyerowitz (London: Peter Owen, 1967), p. 148.

52 Stein, *Everybody's Autobiography*, p. 101.

53 Gertrude Stein, "Two: Gertrude Stein and Her Brother," *Two and Other Early Portraits* (New Haven: Yale University Press, 1951).

54 Gertrude Stein died July 27, 1946. "Two: Gertrude Stein and Her Brother," was published in 1951.

55 Discussing the end of her lecture tour in the United States in 1935, Gertrude Stein wrote in *Everybody's Autobiography*, p. 295:

> Before we went on the Champlain I asked Bennett Cerf about my writing, I always want what I have written to be printed and it has not always happened . . . and now I . . . said something to him, he said it is very simple whatever you decide each year you want printed you tell me and I will publish that thing, just like that I said, just like that, he said, you do the deciding.

This statement coupled with the fact that she had many things printed at her own expense during her lifetime leaves some question about the works she did not choose to have printed.

56 Stein, *Everybody's Autobiography*, p. 76.

57 *Ibid.*, pp. 70-74.

58 Rosalind Miller has published these college themes in *Gertrude Stein: Form and Intelligibility* (New York: Exposition Press, 1949).

59 John Malcolm Brinnin, *The Third Rose: Gertrude Stein and Her World* (Boston: Little, Brown, 1959), pp. 78-82.

60 Stein, *Everybody's Autobiography*, pp. 74-75.

61 *Ibid.*, p. 72.

62 *Ibid.*, p. 76.

63 *Ibid.*, pp. 76-77.

64 Haas and Gallup, *A Catalogue of the Published and Unpublished Writings*, p. 45.

65 This term is defined below. See footnote 66 and page 56.

66 Robert Scholes and Robert Kellogg, *The Nature of Narrative* (New York: Oxford University Press, 1966).

67 That it is indeed the entrance of Alice Toklas is an educated guess. Stein merely adds another "she" here, but I agree with Bridgman, *Gertrude Stein in Pieces*, p. 107, that it is Toklas.

68 Bridgman, *Gertrude Stein in Pieces*, p. 107.

69 It is not being overlooked that the narrator here has done something even more drastic than simply changing his method. He appears to be deliberately confusing, or at least fusing, the identities of the two women in the passage; and his language has become more "difficult" to follow than the earlier section of the portrait. The point is, of course, an important one, but the discussion of it will be held off until it can be compared with the "mask" of narration in *Everybody's Autobiography*, later in this discussion. I am suspending the consideration until that time because *Everybody's Autobiography* contains Stein's use of the first person for autobiographical material and therefore seems a more logical place for comparison with the presentation of those materials presented in third-person narration.

70 Stein, "A Transatlantic Interview," p. 17.

71 Gertrude Stein, "The Portrait of Constance Fletcher,"

Geography and Plays (Boston: Four Seas, 1922). See Haas and Gallup, *A Catalogue of the Published and Unpublished Writings*, p. 45, for a complete listing of these portraits.

72 Miller, *Gertrude Stein*, p. 50.

73 *Ibid.*, p. 50.

74 Stein, "Portraits and Repetitions," p. 171.

75 In this connection consider Gertrude Stein's favorite story about U. S. Grant: "Ulysses Grant says in his memoirs all he learned when he was at school was that a noun is the name of anything, he did not really learn it but he heard it said so often that he almost came to believe it." *Everybody's Autobiography*, p. 200.

76 In Stein, *Everybody's Autobiography*, p. 175, Gertrude Stein relates the following incident about seeing her own name in lights shortly after her arrival back in America:

> . . . and then we went out again on an avenue and the elevated railroad looked just like it had ever so long ago and then we saw an electric sign moving around a building and it said Gertrude Stein has come and that was upsetting. Anybody saying how do you do to you and knowing your name may be upsetting but on the whole it is natural enough but to suddenly see your name is always upsetting. Of course it has happened to me pretty often and I like it to happen just as often but always it does give me a little shock of recognition and nonrecognition. It is one of the things most worrying in the subject of identity.

77 Edith Sitwell, *Aspects of Modern Poetry* (London: Duckworth, 1934), pp. 220-22, says of this portrait that it is not the story, the facts that make it interesting but ". . . the pattern, the rhythm, and the texture. . . ."

78 Bridgman, *Gertrude Stein in Pieces*, pp. 103-04.

79 William Carlos Williams, *The Autobiography of William Carlos Williams* (New York: Random House, 1951), p. 256.

80 Gertrude Stein, "The Portrait of Mabel Dodge at the Villa

Curonia," *Portraits and Prayers* (New York: Random House, 1934). This portrait was first published in June 1913 in *Camera Work*.

81 In "A Transatlantic Interview," p. 18, Stein said:

> After all, human beings are interested in two things. They are interested in the reality and interested in telling about it. I had struggled up to that time with the creation of reality, and then I became interested in how you could tell this thing in a way that anybody could understand and at the same time keep true to your values, and the thing bothered me a great deal at that time.

82 This idea is expanded in the section following.

The Middle Years: 1913-1932

TENDER BUTTONS

Gertrude Stein's middle years — her "painting" period[1] as she called it — were characterized by her absorption in highly experimental fiction. Her works of this period broke with the conventions of nineteenth-century fiction in three major ways: first, her treatment of language as if it were an autotelic rather than a representational entity; second, her treatment of time as if it were pure duration rather than as a category presentable only through spatial metaphors; and third, her treatment of "reality" as if it were not to be imitated but, strictly speaking, "analyzed."

These three ideas are closely related to three great men who dominate the late nineteenth century: Stéphane Mallarmé, Henri Bergson, and Paul Cézanne.[2] The ideas are also important to the twentieth-century Cubist movement in Paris at the turn of the century, of which Gertrude Stein became an intimate a few years after she had settled permanently in that city.

It is not necessary to demonstrate direct influences on Stein, but rather to suggest possible antecedents for those technical innovations so prevalent in the mature narrative prose Gertrude Stein produced during the years 1913-1932.

Stéphane Mallarmé (1842-1898) is Gertrude Stein's most immediate predecessor in the use of words as nonrepresentational entities. Although he was not the first to discover that words have mystical, incantatory powers, he did formulate the notion that words must be disassociated from their conventional grammatical structures in order that they may be freed for new functions, or even freed to exist as ends rather than solely as "means" to "meaning."[3] Words are dynamic, that is, they can generate their own realities. "To speak has no connection with the reality of things," he wrote.[4] Therefore, to use language as if it stood in place of reality is to overlook the idea that all language is metaphor.

We have noted that Gertrude Stein's development during her early years was away from a visible third-person narrator, toward the nonrepresentational use of language. Writing in "Crise de Vers," ("Crisis in Verse") Mallarmé had said:

> The pure work implies the elocutory disappearance of the poet who abandons the initiative to words mobilized by the shock of their inequality; they light one another up with mutual reflections like a virtual trail of fire upon precious stones, replacing the breathing perceptible in the old lyric blast or the enthusiastic personal direction of the phrase. [171]

We will see shortly that allowing words a maximum amount of free play without the intrusion of a visible narrator or a representational organization is an important method in the narrative structure of *Tender*

Buttons[5] — as indeed it is throughout Stein's middle period. However, there are other important ideas to be considered first.

Two ideas of the philosopher Henri Bergson are related to Stein's experimentations: the concept of time as pure duration, and Bergson's conception of the role of intuition in art.

In his *Essai sur les données immédiates de la conscience* (published in English under the title, *Time and Free Will: An Essay on the Immediate Data of Consciousness*),[6] Bergson distinguished between two kinds of time: "the one free from all alloy, the other surreptitiously bringing in the idea of space."[7] Bergson continues,

> Pure duration is the form which the succession of our conscious states assumes when our ego lets itself *live,* when it refrains from separating its present states from its former states. For this purpose it need not be entirely absorbed in the passing sensation or idea: for then, on the contrary, it would no longer *endure.* Nor need it forget its former states: it is enough that, in recalling these states, it does not set them alongside its actual state as one point alongside another, but forms both the past and the present into an organic whole, as happens when we recall the notes of a tune, melting, . . . into one another. [100]

We will see that the works of Gertrude Stein's middle period are marked by what appears to be the absence of any conventional representation of time. However, the absence is not of the element of time or duration in the Bergsonian sense, but rather of the representation of time through the metaphors of space. Stein is attempting during this period to escape the tyranny of the conventional time-line because it is a spatial trap. Bergson wrote: ". . . pure duration might well be nothing but a succession of qualitative changes, which melt into and permeate one another, without precise outlines, without any tendency to externalize themselves in relation to one another, without any affiliation with number: . . . " (104). Therefore, for any writer to utilize a series of events strung out as discrete units in the life of a character was to create a "false sense of time," as Stein was to refer to it many years later.[8]

The second important idea that Bergson formulated was the concept of the role of the intuition as opposed to the intellect. In his *Creative Evolution*[9] Bergson defined the intellect as the fact gatherer. It is the function which allowed the empirical sciences to have developed. But the intellect cannot grasp the inner reality of life because it is "characterized by an inability to comprehend life" (182), because "life transcends the intellect" (34). The intellect then, is concerned with the "outside" of life, while the intuition deals with the inside (194).

The importance of this distinction, coming as it did at a time when a reaffirmation of the value of the individual vision of life was needed,[10] is that it gave the young artists of the period a renewed faith in their roles as creators of their own reality. Bergson wrote,

> Our eye perceives the feature of the living being, merely as assembled, not as mutually organized. The intention of life, the simple movement that runs through the lines, that binds them together and gives them significance, escapes it. This intention is just what the artist tries to regain, in placing himself back within the object by a kind of sympathy, in breaking down, by an effort of intuition, the barrier that space puts up between him and his model. [194]

By applying his sense of the inner movement of life, then, the artist can communicate his own view of reality. This concept was of great importance to the school of art with which Paul Cézanne was identified.

Unlike either Mallarmé or Bergson, Paul Cézanne (along with Flaubert) was spoken of as a direct influence by Gertrude Stein. In *Lectures in America* (1935), she made a comparison between Courbet and Cézanne which had impressed her in her youth:

> But Courbet bothered me. He did really use the color that nature looked like that any landscape looked like when it was just like itself as you saw it in passing. Courbet really did use the colors that nature looked like to anybody, that a water-fall in the woods looked like to anybody.
>
> And what had that to do with anything, in fact did it not destroy a little of the reality of the oil painting. The paintings of Courbet were very real as oil paintings, they existed very really as oil painting, but did the colors that were the colors anybody could see trees and water-falls naturally were, did these colors add or did they detract from the reality of the oil painting as oil painting. [74-75]

In contrast to this impression of Courbet's oil paintings is Stein's description of Cézanne's:

> And then slowly through all this and looking at many many pictures I came to Cezanne. . . . The landscape looked like a landscape that is to say what is yellow in the landscape looked yellow in the oil painting, and what was blue in the landscape looked blue in the oil painting and if it did not there still was the oil painting, the oil painting by Cezanne. The same thing was true of the people there was no reason why it should be but it was, the same thing was true of the chairs, the same thing was true of the apples. The apples looked like apples the chairs looked like chairs and it all had nothing to do with anything because if they did not look like apples or chairs or landscape or people they were apples and chairs and landscape and people. They were so entirely these things that they were not an oil painting and yet that is just what the Cezannes were they were

78

an oil painting. They were so entirely an oil painting that it was all there whether they were finished, . . . or whether they were not finished. . . . it always was what it looked like the very essence of an oil painting because everything was always there, really there. [76-77]

It was, then, not only Cézanne's "composition" which excited Stein, as she had also remarked, but further there was something in Cézanne's work which seemed to her to have captured more than the external reality she had seen captured by Courbet's. Cézanne had caught the very essence of appleness, if you will, so that if his apples did not look like apples they were apples anyway. Conversely, Courbet's apples were not real to her just because, being the apples that any one could see, they lost some of their "reality" for Stein. Cézanne, then, had not imitated reality in the strict representational sense, but had analyzed it.[11] And it is this concept that had so impressed Stein about Cézanne.

The conception was reinforced and further developed by her meeting and long association with the young Cubist painters of the day[12] — especially Pablo Picasso. These young artists had begun gathering in the Montmartre in Paris at about the same time that Gertrude Stein had finished the writing of *Three Lives* (1905). Gertrude and her brother Leo were just then getting seriously involved in their endless visits to Parisian art shops, and their purchases of works by unknown painters.

The meeting between the Steins and the Montmartre group — particularly Picasso — has been variously recorded in many books. It was Leo, apparently, who first "discovered" the young Pablo Picasso. In fact, at first, Gertrude Stein could not bear Picasso's paintings.[13] But something about her face obviously attracted the young Picasso because, although he had not painted a portrait from a model since he was sixteen years old (he was twenty-four when he met Gertrude Stein), he asked her to sit for him, which she did during the winter of 1905-1906.[14]

At these sittings, the two became lifelong friends, and although "she may have been slow in coming to an acceptance and appreciation of the painter's work, . . . when its significance did become apparent to her, his impact on her career was resonant for many years."[15] Picasso became an intimate of the Steins, and the Steins became intimates of the Montmartre group and were therefore involved in the Cubist movement which was just then taking shape in Montmartre.

Writing in 1913, Guillaume Apollinaire attempted to "formulate the new aesthetic values of the day,"[16] in a work entitled, *The Cubist Painters: Aesthetic Meditations.*[17] The work, as the title suggests, deals with the young Cubist painters of the years just before the outbreak of the First World War. Apollinaire says that these young painters were justified in creating a new aesthetic because, "You cannot carry around on your back the corpse of your father" (10). He continues, "It is the social function of great poets and artists to renew continually the appearance nature has for the eyes of men" (14).

This, Apollinaire contends, is just what the young Cubist painters were doing:

> Cubism differs from the old schools of painting in that it aims, not at an art of imitation, but at an art of conception, which tends to rise to the height of creation. [17]

One statement of this new aesthetic is the summary Robert W. Greene has given:

> Cubism as an aesthetic arose out of the growing awareness of these painters of the tremendous gap that separates the artistic representation of an object from its actual structure. For the Cubists ... representation and structure conflict. Since the solidity of things can never be totally reconciled with the picture plane, any attempt to render objective reality through imitation is doomed to failure. ... The Cubists ... thus began painting objects not as they saw them but as they conceived of them. ... [12]

Apollinaire concludes his discussion of the Cubists in general (before discussing them individually):

> The modern school of painting seems to me the most audacious that has ever appeared. It has posed the question of what is beautiful in itself.
> It wants to visualize beauty disengaged from whatever charm man has for man, and until now, no European artist has dared attempt this. The new artists demand an ideal beauty, which will be, not merely the proud expression of the species, but the expression of the universe, to the degree that it has been humanized by light. ... I love the art of today because above all else I love the light, for man loves light more than anything; it was he who invented fire. [18]

Tender Buttons[18] was written by the same year that Guillaume Apollinaire was writing his formulation of the new aesthetics.[19] As we will see, this work contains a view of reality closely related to the Cubist aim of "painting objects not as they saw them but as they conceived of them. ... " The title, *Tender Buttons*, is thus indicative, for this is the first time that Stein used a title which was in itself an indication of the free play of words to follow in the piece. Her previous titles were quite conventional in wording, even if they did not headline conventional works.

The title *Tender Buttons* does indicate the tenor of the work. Buttons are not "tender" in most people's world. The juxtaposition of "tender" with a word like "buttons" presents an intellectual surprise to a reader, and, therefore, forces the reader into a new awareness of linguistic possibilities, which is exactly the *raison* of *Tender Buttons.*

The book was apparently written during a trip to Spain that Gertrude Stein and Alice Toklas took together in 1913. It was not Stein's first trip to Spain, but, coming as it did after several years of friendship with Pablo Picasso, and many other Spanish painters, her new impressions of Spain were greatly heightened. Her perceptions had undergone a complete retraining through her long association with the Montmartre painters. She had been taught to write with her eyes, as she was fond of saying afterward.[20]

Tender Buttons is a slim little book of only seventy-eight pages. It is organized around three major headings: "Objects," "Food," and "Rooms." It has no plot, and no characters, except, of course, a voice speaking about each topic. Although that voice does not, strictly speaking, constitute a narrator if one requires the usual components for a narrator — a story, and a story teller[21] — the voice in *Tender Buttons* will be referred to here as the narrative voice, or simply as the narrator, because in a very real sense what is being communicated in *Tender Buttons* is the struggle of the artist to find the essence of whatever object is being concentrated on at any one moment. It is easier to demonstrate from example. The following are two selections from "Roastbeef":

> Lovely snipe and tender turn, excellent vapor and slender butter, all the splinter and the trunk, all the poisonous darkning

drunk, all the joy in weak success, all the joyful tenderness, all the section and the tea, all the stouter symmetry. [35]

There is no use there is no use at all in smell, in taste, in teeth, in toast, in anything, there is no use at all and the respect is mutual. [35]

While it is obvious from these two selections that the "narrator" here is not telling a story, in the conventional sense, there *is* a sense in which a story *is* being told. Someone is in the presence of a plate of roast beef — that much is certain. Furthermore, that someone is attempting to recreate that roast beef without availing himself of any of the conventional names for its description. In fact, without the title of the section, the reader would have no little trouble in identifying the subject of the two short paragraphs. The narrator, then, is recording something like his own processes of creating. This can be seen from the language employed in the sections. The language leaps into the essence of the roast beef in a joyful, playful, exuberant high concentration on something quite apart from the logical processes ordinarily called into play by roast beef.

The pervasive internal rhyme, one of the self-generative characteristics of autotelic language, is part of this playful joy that takes us far from the drudgery of mere meaning. As in the case of alliteration, once the pattern is begun, the language can itself take over and complete the process. And, of course, through the use of rhyme another dimension is added to the selection — that of a kind of musical sound for its own sake. "All the joy in weak success, all the joyful tenderness. . . ." The language has become almost a song through its autotelic use of the words alone.

If we compare Stein's use of language here to the use of language in a poem by Emily Dickinson, "A Bird Came Down the Walk,"[22] we may, perhaps, gain some insight into Stein's method in the passage quoted above. The following lines are from the Dickinson poem:

> And he unrolled his feathers
> And rowed him softer home
> Than oars divide the ocean,
> Too silver for a seam,
> Or butterflies, off banks of noon,
> Leap, plashless as they swim.

[78-79]

Compare the poetry of Dickinson to the prose of Stein: "Lovely snipe and tender turn, excellent vapor and slender butter, all the splinter and the trunk, all the poisonous darkning drunk. . . ." This thought contains no more conventionally rational "sense" than calling an ocean "too silver for a seam," or describing a take-off site for butterflies as, "off banks of noon."

But there is a tremendous difference here: in the Dickinson poem we have a narrator who at least appears to be viewing an external event; and in the Stein piece the narrator is unconcerned with anybody's reality but his own — or that of the roast beef.

The difference is that in the Stein piece we have what amounts to *de facto* Literary Cubism. "The work of the creative imagination was not to reflect the world but to invent it. Proceeding like blind explorers, the painters invaded the world, so to speak, broke down appearances, and brought to light hidden versions of reality."[23] The stress in this period was on the artist to expose a new and objective reality from the object under consideration. As Donald Sutherland writes:

> ... the subject matter of *Tender Buttons* — objects, food, rooms — was chosen for a definite reason. It corresponds to the 'still life,' the familiar objects on the table top, that were used as basic subject matter by the cubists. As the created reality and not the original reality had to be everything in the cubist picture, the original reality had to be as simple and familiar as possible, to contain nothing but a visual interest and even that visual interest as unprejudiced as possible by tradition.[24]

Consider another example from *Tender Buttons*. The following is a selection from "A Piece of Coffee":

> The settling of stationing cleaning is one way not to shatter scatter and scattering. The one way to use custom is to use soap and silk for cleaning. The one way to see cotton is to have a design concentrating the illusion and the illustration. The perfect way is to accustom the thing to have a lining and the shape of a ribbon and to be solid, quite solid in standing and to use heaviness in morning. It is light enough in that. It has that shape nicely. Very nicely may not be exaggerating. Very strongly may be sincerely fainting. May be strangely flattering. May not be strange in everything. May not be strange to. [12-13]

Isolating the technique of this passage from its meaning for a moment, the reader who will waive the necessity for particular meaning in this passage can easily get caught up in the two devices the narrator is using.

The first device is the linguistic one of the internal vowel changes in echoed words such as "custom," "cotton," and "accustom," in the first four lines. Gertrude Stein spoke of the cinema technique and how it is used to present one frame, slightly different from the next, without exact repetition. The internal vowel change in the passage cited above gives the feeling that the narrator is following some such pattern, when actually he is "free floating" with the language — no longer feeling any representational obligation toward the object. The narrator has abandoned consideration of the *object*, and has gone beyond it into the area of what Malarmé describes as "pure" language.

Much of the same use of language occurs in the repeated alliteration so prevalent in this piece. "The settling of stationing . . . shatter scatter . . . scattering," of the opening line illustrates the point. These words are not so much concerned with the object — coffee — as they are with the unleashing of words with related sounds.

The second device to be examined here is the increasing tempo created by the narrator whose sentences become shorter toward the end. Acceleration is felt also in the repeated use of "may" in such successive, short, alliterated phrases as "very nicely may . . .," "very strongly may . . .," "may be strangely . . .," "may not be strange in . . .," "may not be strange to." It is as if the individuality of the word "may" has become the dominant creative principle, leaving behind the reality of the narrator, *or* the reality of "a piece of coffee."

It is obvious that these linguistic devices do not lead to a clear "picture" of coffee. To the painters and writers of the Cubist period, as well as to the writers of some of the earlier periods, such as Mallarmé, clarity was irrelevant. They were more concerned with capturing a reality they themselves had created. As Gertrude Stein said to Robert Haas, "Picasso said that no one is capable of understanding you who is not capable of doing the same work himself."[25]

No scholar of Gertrude Stein's works has ever

claimed to understand every line she wrote. In fact, some of the works from this middle period are so obscure that not only would the reader have to be "capable of doing the same work himself," but he would also have to know how it feels to be Gertrude Stein staring at coffee or at roast beef in a hotel room with Alice Toklas in Spain in 1913 in order to comprehend the total experience expressed.

That is not, however, a negative criticism of Stein. She was not writing "entertainments." She was creating a new narrative reality which demanded a different mind-set from the reader. Her comments on *Tender Buttons* as a whole, and on individual passages from it, lend insight into her method.

Shortly before her death in 1946, Robert Haas arranged an "interview" with Gertrude Stein, in which she answered several questions. Because the circumstances of this interview were unusual, they are presented here:

> . . . just before communication with France was cut off and for a short time after the war closed, Gertrude Stein and I worked together on our favorite project. It was to be a book. . . .
> It was in preparation for this book that the transatlantic interview came about. Since conversation was, in my opinion, one of Stein's great forms, I believed a substantial sample of her oral pyrotechnics should be included. . . . This was before the time of the tape recorder, and so it was arranged that one of our friends, William S. Sutton, . . . agreed to secure an interview for me. My questions would be mailed to him in Paris . . . he would put them to her, and her answers would be recorded in shorthand and sent to me. . . .[26]

Among the many questions put to Gertrude Stein were some concerning *Tender Buttons,* not only as a whole, but also, and ever more interestingly, some concerning particular portions of the work. Because certain of those segments, with her comments on them, are of conclusive value to the premise of this argument, the rest of the examples from *Tender Buttons* presented here will be only those which she herself chose to comment about — those which contribute to the understanding of the narrative techniques about which we are concerned.

The first comments made by Stein in the interview concern *Tender Buttons* as a whole:

> I was a little obsessed by words of equal value. Picasso was painting my portrait at that time, and he and I used to talk this thing over endlessly. At this time he had just begun on cubism. And I felt that the thing I got from Cézanne was not the last composition. You had to recognize words had lost their value in the Nineteenth Century, particularly towards the end, they had lost much of their variety, and I felt that I could not go on, that I had to recapture the value of the individual word, find out what it meant and act within it. [17-18]

The following selection, "A Little Bit of a Tumbler," from *Tender Buttons,* followed immediately by Gertrude Stein's comments on it, together illustrate her philosophy during this period:

> A shining indication of yellow consists in there having been more of the same color than could have been expected when all four were bought. This was the hope which made the six and seven have no use for any more places and this necessarily spread into nothing. Spread into nothing. [24]

About this passage, she said:

> I have used this idea in more places. I used to take objects on a table, like a tumbler or any kind of object and try to get the picture of it clear and separate in my mind and create a word relationship between the word and the things seen. 'A shining in-

dication of yellow . . .' suggests a tumbler and something in it. '. . . when all four were bought' suggests there were four of them. I try to call to the eye the way it appears by suggestion the way a painter can do it. This is difficult and takes a lot of work and concentration to do it. I want to indicate it without calling in other things. 'This was the hope which made the six and seven have no use for any more places . . . .' Places bring up a reality. '. . . and this necessarily spread into nothing,' which does broken tumbler which is the end of the story. [25]

It is clear from Stein's comments on this selection that she was attempting to release her own mind from previous associations with the isolated, individual words of "A Little Bit of a Tumbler," and with the tumbler itself as an object. In this light, there is a "story" being told by the narrator. It is, in fact, a significant example of a story without any sense of isolated time. From the comments we get the sense that one day she went shopping for tumblers and bought four yellow ones. She brought them home and set them on a table and studied them for a long time. Long concentration on the objects suggested certain words to her. These words were recorded because they seemed to encompass her intuitive response to the tumblers. She did not want to use conventional words to describe them; she wanted to "call to the eye the way it appears by suggestion. . . ."[27] After she had concentrated on the objects long enough for the words necessary for capturing her experience to present themselves, the tumblers "break," "which is the end of the story."

Although Stein does not comment on exactly what causes the tumblers to break, there is the possibility that "reality" intruded, and that is why it all "necessarily spread into nothing." The tumblers did not actually break — they broke metaphorically as her concentration broke. Thus the title "A Little Bit of a Tumbler" — she had grasped in her mind only *a little bit of a tumbler* before the mood was broken and she finished the "exercise."

Return for a moment to the thought that this piece is a good example of a "story" with no sense of isolated time: if it is true that "A Little Bit of a Tumbler" includes all the "events" that Stein mentions in her comments, it is remarkable that there is no time-sense of these events as isolated, or as a "discrete series," in Bergson's phrase. Even though Stein's comments indicate that there is a past, present, and indeed a future implied in the events, there is no distinguishable timeline in the piece itself. The narrator has caught the whole thing at once — as a *duration* in which all timelines become circular, blending and weaving back into themselves. The very first line illustrates the point. "A shining indication of yellow consists in there having been more of the same color than could have been expected when all four were bought." In this one sentence we are given a yellow which is shining, in the present tense, and the present moment. That present moment is juxtaposed immediately with a moment in the past when the object exuding that yellow was bought. The moments are not isolated, they are presented together. The yellow in the present appears stronger than it was thought to be at the moment of purchase — apparently because the observer has studied it much more closely in the isolation of the present moment. Then, in a kind of triumph over time, the piece continues in the past tense which appears to be a *continuation of the present*. The phrase, "and this necessarily spread into nothing," must take place after the yellow has been studied at the present moment, even though a close study of the verb tense would indicate that it *did* "necessarily spread into nothing" in the present/future, so to speak.

We should not leave the discussion of *Tender Buttons* without presenting one more short selection from it. Aside from its being a personal favorite as an example of Gertrude Stein's humor (which does not always receive critical appreciation), it is also a splendid example of her experimentation with the power of word suggestion and association. The following is complete as presented here.

"A White Hunter"

A white hunter is nearly crazy. [24]

These are Stein's comments on this selection:

'A white hunter is nearly crazy.' This is an abstract, I mean an abstraction of color. If a hunter is white he looks white, and that gives you a natural feeling that he is crazy, a complete portrait by suggestion, that is what I had in mind to write. [24]

Stein's comments are almost as funny as the piece itself is. In fact, she has often been attacked by critics simply because her explications are less than explicatory, and some critics see in such an attitude an attack on the whole field of criticism.[28] However, if, as Stein indicates, the idea of white in the selection is an abstraction, then one has only to imagine, for instance, a canvas painted in absolute, stark white to perceive how blinding the picture of a white hunter would look — if the hunter is blinding white, the response would be a "natural feeling that he is crazy."

On another level, that of the play of words, one can see that this very short little piece has a great deal of suggested association. First, there is the idea of the "white hunter," and the connotation of that phrase regarding racial problems. The idea of the white hunter carries with it the implication of the Black as the "white man's burden," with all of the well-known overtones of political attitudes and colonial practices, and, in imagination at least, the big safari hunter with his long lines of black toters. In short, the term instantly calls to mind the big he-man Anglo-Saxon in all his infinite "superiority" over the "inferior" races. To suddenly juxtapose that image with one of his being "nearly crazy" is unexpected and dramatically telling, especially at a time when the image of the white hunter was a positive one in Western culture.[29]

Of course, the real "surprise," as Mallarmé would have said, is that this white hunter is not crazy, he is *nearly* crazy. This qualification presents all kinds of interesting thought associations. What does "nearly" crazy mean? And why is a white hunter *nearly*, and not *simply* crazy? Saying that he is nearly crazy undercuts the pronouncement in such a way that it becomes almost — but not quite — a joke. Can it be that the narrator has also intended to suggest the blinding whiteness of the African sun with his use of "white hunter," and of "crazy"? Perhaps not, but it can surely be argued that no suggestion presented in these words is invalid, since the intent of the narrator is to suggest a "complete portrait" through word association. Therefore, unless there is some reason to limit the associations suggested by the words, there remains an infinite range of possibilities.

The sentence, "A white hunter is nearly crazy," suggests the kind of play and playfulness with language that is employed in *Tender Buttons*. In a way, the accomplishments of that sentence summarize the achievement of *Tender Buttons* as a whole. As Haas has expressed it, "*Tender Buttons* was . . . to Gertrude Stein's development what the 'Demoiselles d'Avignon'[30] was to Picasso's, a key work marked with the enormous struggle of creating a new value."[31]

"VACATION IN BRITANY"

When the First World War broke out in France, Gertrude Stein and Alice Toklas were visiting in England, primarily for the purpose of negotiating (with the "leading English publisher," John Lane)[32] for the British publication of *Three Lives*. They were prevented from returning to France for several weeks because France had declared war and was mobilizing. When at last they were allowed to return to Paris, Gertrude Stein and Alice Toklas bought a Ford from the United States, and did relief work together, delivering hospital supplies throughout France.[33] The fact that they were so involved is of considerable importance to this investigation in that the war may have caused people in America to take a sudden interest in those American artists who were living in the midst of it, and several interested groups in the United States were eager for American involvement. In an effort to popularize the war at home, they publicized whatever contributions were made by famous, or nearly famous, Americans to the war effort abroad. Such interest no doubt explains why Mildred Aldrich's two little books[34] about her experiences in the war zone became immediate best sellers in the United States.[35] It is also probably the reason why Gertrude Stein suddenly appeared in such widely different publications as the *New York Sun, Life, Vanity Fair, Broom,* and the *Little Review.*[36]

Another reason for mention of these war years is that Stein wrote nothing of any length during that time. This fact explains the hiatus in this book between *Tender Buttons,* written in 1913, and the next work to be discussed, "Vacation in Britany,"[37] written in 1920,[38] and published in 1922.

Because "Vacation in Britany" is a classic of Gertrude Stein's "painting period," and because until recently it has not been reprinted since its 1922 publication and is unfamiliar to most readers, the work is given here in its entirety.[39]

VACATION IN BRITANY

KING OR KANGAROO KING OR YELLOW. KING OR MARIE CLAIRE SUGGESTS A MEADOW. AND THE USE OF THOUGHT

BY THE SEA

By the sea inland smell the goose, by the figs George buy the figs. By the crown, Sylvester has the crown and glory constant glory. And in the midst of the speed in the rising of the stones stones do not rise of themselves unless they are made to resemble the wood in the midst of stones and salt can we can we declare when a house was built. A house is built either in the shape of a lamb of a heart or of a bush. And almost immediately the walls scale. They whiten and the sun changes chinese red to blue.

Immerse yourself.

LEAVES ME LEAVES ME

Why can you muster men and birds. Why can you whistle so shyly. And why do you mention harm. No eyes can make thirds and no rabbits can cheer. It does them good to be sold. Who sells hens. Connect the impression that earliness and repetition and even octagons are necessary to families. Families really need a fern. Ferns are really seen by their leaves. Whole dogs have trimming. They trim their size. One cannot be merry in peace. And in war. Who can care to wear what is there and in there. Who can carry a nest to the hay. Who can say yes how do you do yesterday. Can you have lettuce, can you have the best figs in a servant.

To serve in a sieve and a saint. To paint and to see all the sea. To see electricity.

CONSCIENCE

Racket is a noise. Noise is a poise. Boys with the b spelled like a p is poise. Boys is poise.

And then I read the men. Men say. Leave me and be gay. Men say tenderness to-day. Men say go away.

And leave me.

A potato field and the promised land. It is a very pleasant burning smell.

Armandine Armandine yesterday noon. Armandine Armandine what is the tune.

Devotion. What is devotion. He is devoted to that. She is devout. And an opening. An opening is covered by Caesars. Sharp wire. Do sharpen wire. Devotion. Devotion is determined by design.

When this you see remember me.

I do mean to replace crockery with furniture. I do mean to organise victory. I do mean to say grace.

I am not a bar tender.

Automatically but not silently.

Little fool little stool little fool for me. Little stool little fool little stool for me. And what is a stool. That was the elegant name for a cow. Little stool little fool little stool for me. Little fool little stool for me.

Let us let us conscience.

Let us let us conscientiously renounce the sense of reticence.

GERTRUDE STEIN

That this short piece is a classic in the middle period of Gertrude Stein's writings can readily be seen in the fact that this narrator is not concerned with the external realities apparent to anyone living in Britany.[40] The narrator *is* concerned with combinations of words, juxtapositions of generally unexpected images, and a wide-ranging freedom to simply "play" with the whole idea of a "Vacation in Britany."

It would be valuable here, before analyzing the piece more carefully, to consider some of Stein's comments about this kind of word-play. She had been charged often enough with writing nonsense by both the public and her critics, and her own comments are germane to the matter.

> While during that middle period I had these two things that were working back to the compositional idea, the idea of portraiture and the idea of the recreation of the word. I took individual words and thought about them until I got their weight and volume complete and put them next to another word, and at this same time I found out very soon that there is no such thing as putting them together without sense. It is impossible to put them together without sense. I made innumerable efforts to make words write without sense and found it impossible. Any human being putting down words had to make sense out of them.[41]

"Immerse yourself," the narrator says at the end of the first paragraph of "Vacation in Britany." Immerse yourself in the scene, in the experience, and then in the recreation of them through the recreation of the word. From the very first paragraph the narrator is attempting to capture some of the important properties of the experience in which he finds himself. "By the sea inland smell the goose . . . ," indicates the method of this first paragraph: the juxtaposition of unrelated objects in order to "restore the sense of immediate unprepared experience," as Donald Sutherland said.[42] To any person who has grown up on the seashore, the call to stand by "the sea inland and smell the goose," is a totally unexpected combination. One expects to smell the salt air, the pungency of rotting seaweed, or dead fish; but one is surprised by the smell of goose at the seashore. Therefore, it is clear that this narrator is not really interested in "How I Spent My Summer Vacation." In fact, the chances are certain that a vacation on any seashore is *not* the topic here. This narrator is at a seashore, immersing himself; but he is immersing himself in language, *not* in objects.

Consider the minute difference in the visual appearance of the word, "island," and "inland," for example. Most people familiar with seashores tend to misread the opening phrase, "By the sea inland," as "By the sea island." The unexpected *in*land instead of *is*land stops the eye at once. The point is that there is only a one letter difference in the two words. Why did the narrator chose "inland" then? Precisely for the reason that it is more useful because unconventional in this context and at the same time so close to the expected word in appearance. It surprises! But, it does more than just surprise: it is an arresting use of self-generative language. The word "island," suggests, by involution, the word "inland," and it is one dimension of the play of language that certain words naturally suggest others, whether or not those words are related to the *meaning* of the sentence. They are related to the sentence, not through meaning, but through rational association with other words which they themselves have generated.

The same kind of play occurs in the phrase "by the

figs George buy the figs." Not only are figs themselves another surprise at the seashore, but the switch from "by" to "buy" serves to keep the concentrating mind open to the nuances of meaning by never allowing it a direct conventional experience. Consider the devices in the very next sentence: it appears that the technique just used will be repeated; it invites the mind to believe it has recognized a pattern of homophones. "By the figs George buy the figs." Then, "By the crown" — and the mind looks for the repeated pattern. But it is not repeated. "By the crown, Sylvester has the crown," and the narrator has suddenly switched his focus and plays with crown, finishing it with "the crown and the glory constant glory." This phrase is interesting, too, because it has the weighty ring of a Shakesperian soliloquy — "the crown and the glory constant glory." It is strangely out of place in the seashore picture.

Then, with the suddenness of the other switches in imagery, the movement appears to return to recognizable objects ... houses and steeply rising stones — possibly stone farm houses, and the salt that would most likely be found on them near the seashore. "The walls scale" — that is, they reach to the sky, and "they whiten." As they reach the sky "the sun changes chinese red to blue," and again it all appears to be a painting, but *this* painting has been done with *two* senses — sight and smell.

In the second paragraph the technique shifts to the use of primarily visual nouns. Stein uses the juxtaposition of unrelated, and therefore unexpected, nouns again in this paragraph; but the use this time is for visual effect, and not for appeal to other senses, as was the case in the first paragraph. The first few lines of the second paragraph contain many farmyard references such as birds, rabbits, hens, and, "it does them good to be sold." She sets up the expectation of some imminent reference to farms. But when the reference does come, it is not to farms at all, but to something entirely different — "Families really need a fern." There can be little doubt that the juxtaposition of fern against the expectation of "farm" has been done by the narrator in order to keep his mind free of previous experience and association with "hens," and "rabbits" and other farmyard suggestions. It is as if this narrator were intentionally leading expectation in one direction for the sole purpose of surprising it into a new reality.

Another matter for consideration in this paragraph is that even when Gertrude Stein is most noticeably "writing with her eyes," there is often internal rhyme, such as "Who can care to wear what is there," combined with other linguistic devices such as the alliteration of "To serve in a sieve and a saint," and homophones "to see all the sea." Obviously there is something happening here other than the heavy appeal to perceptions of color and smell given us in paragraph one. These linguistic devices of the second paragraph most likely serve a particular and important function here. The narrator has foregone the use of intellectual identity between one object and another and, therefore, feels the need to provide *some* connection between the objects lest all communication break down. In lieu of intellectual identity, then, the narrator has substituted a linguistic identity, created through the use of rhyme, alliteration, and homophones.

Consider the three sentences which end the paragraph: "To serve in a sieve and a saint. To paint and to see all the sea. To see electricity." All three linguistic devices are present in this passage. There is no immediate intellectual connection between "serve," "sieve," and "saint." However, a logical alliterative connection is established. The fact that this alliteration is again picked up in the homophones "see," and "sea," is a brilliant combination echoing "serve," "sieve," and "saint," concluding with the "s" sound of "electricity."

The important point is that the narrator is not concerned with making "sense." He is utilizing any device of sight, smell, and linguistic play for the purpose of creating something *like* the experience he himself is having while "feeling" a new essence on this vacation, on this seashore.

The third paragraph shows still another shift. It begins with a syllogism meant, on one level, to display the disdain of the narrator for the strictly intellectual processes. "Racket is a noise. Noise is a poise. Boys with the b spelled like a p is poise. Boys is poise." The narrator then turns back to the painting which began the piece, and appealing again to sight and smell says, "A potato field and the promised land. It is a very pleasant burning smell." Then the paragraph returns to the emphasis on linguistic device, seen in paragraph two, and becomes a riot of linguistic fun.

There is, however, a more serious level on which the syllogism of this paragraph must be explored. It will be recalled that the first paragraph contained very small differences in words: we saw "island" changed to "inland"; we saw the homophones "by," and "buy." In paragraph three, the technique turns to the syllogistic form. The first term of the syllogism is understood immediately: "Racket is a noise." Again, as in the case of the previous paragraphs, the mind is prepared for a quite conventional pattern or approach. And, as with the previous paragraphs, expectation is surprised. The second element of the syllogism here is, "noise is a poise." That is *not* immediately grantable, and was obviously not intended by the narrator as an intellectual recognition. It is a perfectly serious linguistic play. It is also an internal rhyme which functions to draw the mind more deeply into concentration on the language itself, away, for the moment, from the contemplation of the canvas being painted. When that canvas is returned to, it becomes both visual and a riot of lyric.

Taken as a whole, then, "Vacation in Britany" is a study in the creation of new uses for words. It is an attempt to communicate a landscape of sea and rural scene by a narrator who has just created, or *invented*, an idiosyncratic reality out of that landscape. "Vacation in Britany," of course, contains some of the linguistic devices found in *Tender Buttons;* but, "Vacation in Britany" is obviously an attempt to communicate more complicated insights and responses than those created in the "still life" objects Stein used in *Tender Buttons.*

"MADE A MILE AWAY"

"Made a Mile Away"[43] was written in 1924[44] and published in 1927. The title of this ten-page piece tells us that Gertrude Stein proposed to write, from some distance, from "a mile away," about all the pictures she had ever seen which interested her. In her own words Stein describes her intent:

> I once wrote something called Made a Mile Away, which was a
> description of all the pictures that had influenced me, all the

pictures up to this moment the moment when I became familiar with pictures.[45]

It is fascinating to examine what language a writer who "paints with language" uses to describe actual paintings. (The next selection, "Jane Heap," describes a *person* using this technique.)

Essentially, "Made a Mile Away" is unintelligible — for two reasons.

Gertrude Stein has attempted the methodology of painting to describe an intellectual idea — the influence that certain paintings had on her. Nowhere in the work is any painting actually mentioned by name; therefore the reader infers that Stein is discussing a particular painter. The opening sentences are offered in illustration:

Made a mile away.
Description of all the pictures that have attracted some attention.
First Millet. Several miles away or a description.
Juan and Juanita.
First Millet. Thirty miles away as thirty miles away.
Juan and Juanita very differently in a place.
As to places.
Millet as to places.
Juan and Juanita and not as to places.
Millet so much.
Millet so much.
Millet so much Millet so much.
Juan and Juanita for the sake of measure. To measure a settler safely. Juan and Juanita in the past time.
And caring.
Millet has no other father has no other sister has no other either. Millet has no other or either as he has no other. As he has no other.
Juan and Juanita establishes. Juan and Juanita establishes

grain and furs and less and silver and as you call and as you call it and so very much and as much and meaning and in enterprise and for a place and finally and as it has. [155]

It is clear that the narrator appears to be sharing some thoughts about Millet which are very personal. While *suggestion* can be most effective when a narrator attempts to invent a reality dealing with the sensual (such as a seashore experience) this method, when applied to an intellectual idea is a very difficult one to manage. It might be that something could be made of the above passage by piecing together bits of information Gertrude Stein has written elsewhere[46] concerning the influence of specific painters on her. But, after all, most of those bits of information were written many years after "Made a Mile Away," so it can be assumed with some justification that the narrator of "Made a Mile Away" expected this piece to stand on its own merits, without need of additional information. The fact that it is unintelligible without information from outside, indicates that the narrator was not concerned with making his ideas clear to a reader. The narrator appears, rather, to be summoning those very private ideas out of his own mind — to examine his own thoughts — regardless of whether those thoughts would be shared.

The second reason why this work fails to communicate is due, most likely, to the strange device of using color to describe color. Stein had used that technique in *Tender Buttons,* in the sentence, "A white hunter is nearly crazy," but in that sentence the color "white" is used as an adjective to describe "hunter." In "Made a Mile Away," Stein uses colors as nouns — which contributes to the ineffectiveness of the work.

Consider the following example. The narrator introduces this passage with the words, "Among the influences that have made me what I am" (163).

> The first thing that is to be noticed is grey and green. The next thing to be noticed is green and blue, the next thing to be noticed is blue and brown, the next thing to be noticed is brown and black and the next thing to be noticed is black and red. So much to notice. So much notice. To notice so much. [163]

A listing of colors in this manner communicates little of their reality to the reader. The narrator, therefore, appears to be trying to recall something of the importance of these colors to himself — always to himself. It cannot be thought that this narrator seriously intends to recreate anything for his reader. It is much too private.

The final illustration from "Made a Mile Away" has been chosen because of its similarity in alliterative usage to "Vacation in Britany," but with a completely different result. In describing El Greco's influences, the narrator says,

> . . . El Greco. Found by itself as if it were as if it was, it was, it was found by itself and not so for so and as so as so much. Longer so much longer and so much. So much longer and so much and Anthony and so much. So much so and so much. Anthony and as not so much longer. So much longer and seen, feel seen fell seen, fell saw saw it saw him, saw him sell him, see him, seen. As seen a scene. So and seen, seen so, seen as as much longer and seen as so much and as seen and so long. Not good-bye but so long. Longhi. Very nice and quiet I thank you. [156]

For many readers this kind of writing communicates nothing, because far from being "made a mile away," this discussion of El Greco's influences is so close to the narrator's reality that it is almost totally hidden from the reader's. Even though the linguistic devices used in this passage were employed more or less successfully in other pieces — most notably in "Vacation in Britany," to substitute for "sense" — these devices, when used on subject matter with which the reader has no previous experience, cannot enlighten. When one has finished reading "Vacation in Britany," for example, one knows quite a bit about the things at the seashore which influenced the narrator. When one has finished reading the above passage, one knows no more about El Greco's influence on the narrator than one did before reading it.

"Made a Mile Away," has not been chosen as a negative example of Stein's middle period, but as an illustration that points to the probable reason for her choice of landscapes, objects, and people as topics for the exploration and development of this technique. Writing with one's eyes cannot be successful, no matter what linguistic devices are employed, if one's primary goal is the discussion of intellectual ideas.

"J. H. JANE HEAP"

"J. H. Jane Heap,"[47] a five-hundred-word portrait, was written in 1928[48] and published in 1929. Although it was actually written shortly after *Lucy Church Amiably*,[49] it is discussed before *Lucy Church Amiably* because "Jane Heap" offers interesting contrasts to "Made a Mile Away."

Just as "Made a Mile Away" was a portrait of an idea, "Jane Heap" is an interesting example of Stein's "painting" technique applied to the portrait of a person. *Lucy Church Amiably* — a book-length work —

105

is a combination of ideas, landscapes, and persons, and so it will be illuminating to examine a short attempt such as "Jane Heap" first.

Jane Heap was coeditor (with Margaret Anderson)[50] of the *Little Review,* which published many of Gertrude Stein's short works, including Jane Heap's own portrait, subtitled, "Fairly Well, An Appreciation of Jane."

The portrait contains an interesting combination of the devices of repetition (which Stein used extensively in her early period), and the disassociation of words to create a new reality (a device she used often during her "painting period"). Blending the two devices to describe a person makes an interesting experiment.

The opening two paragraphs of the portrait illustrate these devices:

> He seemed that anybody is all of that ordinary come from arrangement agate a gate and tree and she looks like Grace which is true. There are three of them that look like Grace Grace and Brake and many many use to be all gold used to be all gold where it is digging as a predeliction it is an elimination elevation partial periodic objection to pine trees selling call use it but theirs is that a plenty of cutting makes meals a suggestion of what and the evening she came in the evening and she stayed late and the morning she came and stayed late in the evening. She came and stayed late the first time in the evening in the morning she left to stay late in the morning. This is was just the first time. This all to say that Jane Heap any way did stay late the first time in the morning and the evening. She came in the evening and she stayed late and the morning she came and stayed late in the evening. How sweet it is and yet how bitter and it is might is right. She might be right. This is what there is to say to Jane Heap just at break of day in the morning. Jane Heap the first day stayed late in the evening. Fairly well is very good.

Jane Jane come away let the garden come and stay came late to stay in the morning came late to stay the first day in the evening. [9]

Interest is generated immediately because the narrator is combining alliteration in the first part of this passage with the repetition of an apparently factual incident in the life of the subject.[51] The combination results in the total unintelligibility of the first part as compared with the stark simplicity of the repeated "She came in the evening and stayed late in the morning" of the latter part. Then, of course, the narrator almost sings the nursery-rhyme-like "Jane Jane come away. . . ."

The remainder of the portrait is a riot of internal rhyme with which the narrator appears to be having a great deal of linguistic fun. Apparently Jane Heap enjoyed the fun, because she published the piece. The point is that this portrait is a combination of several techniques we have seen Gertrude Stein employ before, but never all together as they are used in this portrait.

These many devices culminate in *Lucy Church Amiably.*

LUCY CHURCH AMIABLY

The great repository of all the narrative techniques Gertrude Stein experimented with during her "painting period" is the long "narrative" work, *Lucy Church Amiably,*[52] written in 1927,[53] and published in 1930. Stein described this work on the title page as "A Novel of Romantic beauty and nature and which Looks Like an Engraving."

Like so many of Stein's works, *Lucy Church Amiably* has been very difficult to obtain. One thousand copies were printed privately in 1930, and until recently the book was not reprinted. Because so few people have had an opportunity to read this novel, numerous illustrations from it are presented.

From the title, it is immediately apparent that Stein has written a work in which word combinations are surprising. Native speakers of English do not commonly use adverbs to modify nouns, but the idiosyncratic use of the adverb in the title sets an important tone for the work as a whole.

By way of an introduction to the book, Stein wrote an "Advertisement" for it, which appears at the beginning. It is quoted in full here because it aids in the general understanding of the work:

> Lucy Church Amiably. There is a church and it is in Lucey and it has a steeple and the steeple is a pagoda and there is no reason for it and it looks like something else. Beside this there is amiably and this comes from the paragraph.
>
> Select your song she said and it was done and then she said and it was done with a nod and then she bent her head in the direction of the falling water. Amiably.
>
> This altogether makes a return to romantic nature that is it makes a landscape look like an engraving in which there are some people, after all if they are to be seen there they feel as pretty as they look and this makes it have a river a gorge an inundation and a remarkable meadowed mass which is whatever they use not to feed but to bed cows. Lucy Church Amiably is a novel of romantic beauty and nature and of Lucy Church and John Mary and Simon Therese.

The advertisement establishes the fact that this work is not a novel in the conventional sense, since it does not have a plot as such, although it does exhibit the "external characteristics of a novel."[54] Essentially, the work is somewhat in the nature of a protracted mural, like the one of the Battle of Waterloo, which Gertrude Stein loved so much as a child in Oakland, California.[55] *Lucy Church Amiably* is a series of landscapes, and of characters in relation to those landscapes, placed in position each to the other.

The book consists of forty-nine chapters. Throughout the first half, the chapters tend to be from twenty to thirty pages in length. Those of the second half are much less consistent, running from several pages to only one sentence.[56]

The first chapter, "Begins the Middle of May," opens with a narrator who is a parody of the third-person objective voice. He appears to be describing the events of a traditional summer vacation (such as Stein was enjoying when she wrote the work).[57] The narrator begins:

> There were as many chairs there and there were two a chair that can be found everywhere a rocking chair that is to say a rocking chair can be found everywhere. Two there at one end and the other at the other end. They were in front of the building and in sitting and rocking there was a very slight declivity in front of the building. [9]

Upon this scene of the rocking chairs in front of some building, there arrive a husband and wife who sit in the chairs. At that point, the narrator takes a side track which has become familiar to readers of Gertrude Stein: when a character is introduced, the narrator presents a short portrait of that character regardless of whether the character has any recognizable importance to the "story." In fact, in the course of the first four pages of *Lucy Church Amiably,* the narrator presents at least six different people, who are described at some length, but who never reappear in the work. This device is used not to suggest that the characters bear any traditional relationship to the plot, but simply to indicate that they are a part of the surrounding landscape. One of the earliest such examples in the work is the following:

> Mr. and Mrs. Paul Daniel went to a part of the country which when it was in apparent order was not only acceptable but convenient they hoped there to find a house which would be suited to them and there not considered familiarly it would be best not to have them visiting. Not at all as rubbish. It is very well known that earlier those who were not satisfied with best left alone were accustomed to be let alone. There has been more nearly sensitiveness equally distributed than either she or they admit. Admittedly.
>
> There can be no inheritance of the jewels as well as the case even if both have been and are to be sold. And replaced by bronze of which there is no particular concerning which there is no particular oratory. Roses open. [10-11]

The passage illustrates two important things about the nature of this narrator: first, he appears to be telling a story. The people mentioned at the opening of the paragraph appear to evoke some recollection in the mind of the narrator — Mr. and Mrs. Daniel *do* something — they go to a certain part of the country. Then, from the particular, the narrator is moved to generalize about "those who were not satisfied. . . ." The generalization in turn leads from people to certain events concerning some jewels. Up to this point the pacing has been very slow, the sentences short, the tone leisurely. Slowly the narrator has led himself to a sudden discovery: "roses open." The curt, unexpected phrase, wholly unanticipated in this context, produces

roses which open before one's startled eyes. We are re-
minded of Mallarmé's notion that a light in a dark room
is more effective than a light in a sunlit room.[58]

The second aspect of this narrator is that he relies upon the "immerse yourself" method of "Vacation in
Britany." That is, if one examines the flow of ideas in
the last paragraph above, one sees that "jewels" and
"inheritance" and "case" and "sold" could easily be
involved in a story about someone. Those objects, combined as they are with the ideas of inheritance and
something being sold, are just on the periphery of
meaning: the entire first line of that second paragraph
consists of perfectly sound English structure and usage.
There is no idiosyncratic element in the sentence, as
there is in the use of the adverb "amiably" to describe
the noun Lucy Church, in the title, and English structure has in no way been "bent" in that first sentence.
What is idiosyncratic is that the use of the causal relationship, while appearing to be the very thing that
gives the sentence recognizable meaning, is the very
thing that undercuts it, and forces the reader to return
to the sentence. Consider again, "There can be no inheritance of the jewels as well as the case *even if* both
have been and are to be sold." [Italics mine.] Had the
sentence read "because" instead of "even if" there
would be the more expected causal relationship.
However, it does not read "because," and, therefore,
the relationship between the two elements becomes
surprising, and, furthermore, even though the sentence
is rationally structured, the surprise of the causal relationship between the elements in it causes the reader to
be "jerked" from its meaning at the last moment. The
point is that the narrator is again "playing," except that

this time he is playing with the balance between juxtaposed ideas rather than the balance between juxtaposed objects, such as "seashore" and the smell of "goose," as he did in "Vacation in Britany." (In Stein's "return to narrative," as she called the writings of her later period, we will see her play with juxtaposition and balance of "time" words to produce surprise, especially in *Ida,* and *Mrs. Reynolds.*)

However, when the narrator turns from playing to other considerations, we see a different kind of immersing. We know that Stein used color rather ineffectively in "Made a Mile Away." *Lucy Church Amiably,* however, contains some of the most effective use of color to be encountered in Stein's works. The following paragraph displays this use of color — and some additional uses of linguistic devices — which make it worth quoting in full.

> Imagining that it would be that he having her she not having other than they they being left in and about and if he were useful usefully could it be that the only desirability would be returned as if not having left for eighteen months while they were leaving it as if in some to taste winter is as might it be enjoyed. All gold is put into water and all water is put into butter and all butter is put into apples and all apples are put into trees and all trees are put into flourishing and all flourishing is put into welcome and all welcome is put into translation and all translation is resisting to their having felt that it was most and best and called called it at the time that it was actually reunited in spite of their addition of which and whether it is mine . . . . [12-13]

The narrator in the above passage is immersing himself in language. Again, the pacing is slow and the sentences long. But this time, the apparent reference to characters at the beginning of the passage leads the narrator into a beautifully provocative non sequitur, ". . . as if not having left for eighteen months while they were leaving it as if in some to taste winter is as might it be enjoyed." These words do not *mean* anything — they entice one (including the narrator) into the winter colors and images which follow. And that, of course, is the whole idea behind the play of language, or its autotelic use. Words leap from one to another — they suggest one another, until, at last, it seems almost as if the author himself has disappeared. Consider the reechoing "l" sound in the remainder of the above paragraph. The sounds generate each other, resulting in what may be called a powerful pastoral song.[59] "All gold . . . all butter . . . all apples . . . all flourishing . . . all welcome. . . ." The narrator is immersing himself in a painting which sings, just as he was immersing himself in a painting which could be smelled in "Vacation in Britany."

This method can be seen again in the sentence, "An orange bee on pink clover and a white butterfly flying well and high over the center of a wide river" (67). We see the pacing of the action evolve slowly enough to allow complete immersion in the idiosyncratic use of color. The passage is completely visual — "orange bee . . . pink clover . . . white butterfly" — but not representational. On the other hand, through the skillful use of pacing in the second part of the sentence, the narrator creates an apparently logical event: ". . . and a white butterfly flying very well and high over the center of a wide river." The use of nonrepresentational color, then, is made to appear *rational* and quite commonplace, because the rest of the *picture* is so *reasonable*. The total picture which emerges from the image is one of slow, almost indolent, summer insects flying high on a summer day. One almost forgets that the insects themselves are far from real.

One additional example should be enough to establish the use of color as an important narrative device in this work.

> Lucy Church was in one at a time and meant to be pleasantly in place of having it this time and once at a time once at a time and not left when they were to them. Lucy Church is indebted to rain for her belief in white and pink. Pink and it might be when it is ordinarily theirs to be sure. It is not only because but with it at once that they choose them and say how do you do. A father quite as much a father quite as much and she quite as much a father quite as much. [87-88]

Lucy Church Amiably represents the culmination of Gertrude Stein's "painting" period. Her use of language in this period is the language of one writing with her eyes, because her purpose and principal interest during these years was the creation, or invention, of a new reality seen through creation of a new value for words.

The measure of Stein's preoccupation with redefining the landscapes, and the churches and people in them in this work, is testified to by the fact that two of the three major critics who have written any assessment at all of *Lucy Church Amiably* seem to find some urgency in suggesting that Gertrude Stein *is* Lucy Church.[60] Such an insistence seems to miss the point of what the narrator is attempting to do. He is immersing himself. Like the cubist painters of the era, the interpreting artist — the creator of the work — finds the question of the reality of the subject, as seen externally, irrelevant. The important goal is the creator's ability to communicate some truth — which is, after all, intensely internal.

There are two other narrative devices in *Lucy Church Amiably* deserving of mention: the mural in relation to this work, and Stein's employment of a kind of nursery song in "Jane Jane come away . . ." from the portrait, "Jane Heap." Stein uses the same kind of sing-song chant in *Lucy Church Amiably* often enough to suggest the movement from one frame to another of a mural. For example, the song of the American soldiers from World War I — "Left right left, I had a good job and I left," Stein changes to, "In this way introduced to left left left right left" (13). The point is that the topic often changes when that phrase is used, giving the suggestion of eye movement from one center of interest to another, as in a mural.

Many times in Stein's writing one comes across a reference to the nursery rhyme, "One two three four, shut the door." And it is present frequently in *Lucy Church Amiably*. The following example combines both the soldier's chant and the use of numbers:

> Who knows the difference between once and twice and John Mary interchanges left to right. Interchanges. Very quickly interchanges might leave it to them with them he leaving with them with them in place of eight and forty two. It is very noticeable that is she sits and rests it is very much a very great pleasure to observe her.
> 2.30, 3.30, 4.30, 5.30, 6.30, 7.30, 8.30. It is not easy to be seen wishing when the water is noisy. [65-66]

Lucy Church Amiably was the last long prose work in Stein's middle period. In it she brought to fruition many of the techniques and interests we saw emerging toward the end of her early years. Although in the

1930s her interests turned away from the nonrepresentational use of language toward what she termed going "back to the form of narration,"[61] she did not altogether, ever, forgo the interplay of alliteration and rhyme. These devices recur throughout the remainder of her career.

NOTES

1 Gertrude Stein, *Everybody's Autobiography* (New York: Random House, 1937), p. 180.

2 It is not my intention to categorically dismiss other great thinkers of the nineteenth century — such as the British and American Empiricists, or William James, whom Gertrude Stein admired greatly. I am rather suggesting that for the Cubist movement as a whole in Paris at the turn of the century the three names I have suggested here play a more immediate role.

3 I am indebted to Professor Gayatri C. Spivak for this discussion.

4 Stéphane Mallarmé, "Crisis in Verse," *Mallarmé*, trans. Anthony Hartley (Baltimore: Penguin Books, 1965), p. 171.

5 For a different approach to the analysis of *Tender Buttons* see Allegra Stewart, "Selfhood and the Word," in *Gertrude Stein and the Present* (Cambridge: Harvard University Press, 1967), pp. 69-139.

6 Henri Bergson, *Time and Free Will: An Essay on the Immediate Data of Consciousness*, trans. F. L. Pogson (New York: Macmillan, 1928). This work was first published in French in 1889.

7 *Ibid.*, p. 100.

8 Gertrude Stein, "A Transatlantic Interview," in *Gertrude Stein, A Primer for the Gradual Understanding of Gertrude Stein*, ed. Robert Bartlett Haas (Los Angeles: Black Sparrow Press, 1971), p. 20.

9 Henri Bergson, *Creative Evolution*, trans. Arthur Mitchell (New York: Modern Library, 1944).

10 I am indebted to Edmund Wilson, *Axel's Castle* (New York:

Charles Scribner's Sons, 1945) for a discussion of this matter.

11 I am indebted to Roger Fry, *Cézanne: A Study of His Development* (New York: Macmillan, 1927) for his discussion of Cézanne's contributions to the twentieth century.

12 See Georges Lemaitre, *From Cubism to Surrealism in French Literature* (New York: Russell and Russell, 1967); and, Cecily Mackworth, *Guillaume Apollinaire and the Cubist Life* (New York: Horizon Press, 1963) for excellent discussions of the painters and writers of this period in Paris.

13 John Malcolm Brinnin, *The Third Rose: Gertrude Stein and Her World* (Boston: Little, Brown, 1959), pp. 70-71.

14 *Ibid.*, pp. 71-73.

15 *Ibid.*, p. 71.

16 Robert W. Greene, *The Poetic Theory of Pierre Reverdy* (Berkeley: University of California Press, 1967), p. 11.

17 Guillaume Apollinaire, *The Cubist Painters: Aesthetic Meditations*, trans. Lionel Abel (New York: Wittenborn, Schultz, 1949).

18 Gertrude Stein, *Tender Buttons* (New York: Claire Marie Press, 1914).

19 For the difficulties involved in dating the writing of this work precisely, see Allegra Stewart, *Gertrude Stein and the Present*, p. 75.

20 Stein, "A Transatlantic Interview," p. 31.

21 Robert Scholes and Robert Kellogg, *The Nature of Narrative* (New York: Oxford University Press, 1966), p. 240.

22 Emily Dickinson, "A Bird Came Down the Walk," in *Poems by Emily Dickinson*, eds. Martha Dickinson Bianchi and Alfred Leete Hampson (Boston: Little, Brown, 1942), pp. 78-79.

23 Brinnin, *The Third Rose*, p. 128.

24 Donald Sutherland, *Gertrude Stein: A Biography of Her Work* (New Haven: Yale University Press, 1951), pp. 85-86.

25 Stein, "A Transatlantic Interview," p. 33.

26 Robert Haas, ed., *A Primer for the Gradual Understanding of Gertrude Stein*, p. 13.

27 One recalls here the distinction Stein made between the Courbet and the Cézanne oil paintings. Courbet's "detracted from the reality" of their subject matter by being too faithful to the surface reality which anyone could see and recognize. The paintings of Cézanne, on the other hand, captured for Stein something beneath or beyond the surface reality so that it became irrelevant whether the object was recognizable. The apple was an apple whether it looked like one or not.

28 The documentation for this statement could run for several pages with names of critics who have taken exception to Stein's explications. However, one critic who seems to be especially angry with her is Wyndham Lewis. See his "Preface," *Time and Western Man* (Boston: Beacon Press, 1957), pp. x-xi.

29 This was the era of the colonial attitudes expressed in Joseph Conrad's, *Heart of Darkness,* for example. These ideas continued to be expressed, of course, as late as Ernest Hemingway's African stories.

30 Cecily Mackworth, *Guillaume Apollinaire and the Cubist Life,* p. 83, discusses the importance of this painting to Picasso's development:

> Les Demoiselles d'Avignon had nothing to do with Beauty and could not have been called beautiful by any standards. When he painted the picture, Picasso had been trying to achieve something else, something quite different. For the first time, perhaps, since the Renaissance a painter had refused to content himself with remaining in front of his subject and considering it from a single angle. He had treated the five figures in the picture as palpable objects, with numerous surfaces or facets, all of which could be 'possessed' by the painter, merely by changing his own position instead of remaining immobile at a respectful distance. In this way, he had shown the component parts of the whole, instead of just those which would have come within a single angle of vision. The picture represented for the first time, instead of a desire to create Beauty, a conscious triumph of Will

over Taste. It had been conceived out of the painter's desire to discover the truth about a given object by revealing simultaneously all its aspects or angles, as if he was placed, not in front of his subject, but at its very center.

31 Stein, "A Transatlantic Interview," p. 23.

32 See, Gertrude Stein, *The Autobiography of Alice B. Toklas* (New York: Harcourt, Brace, 1933), pp. 176-80, for details of this visit.

33 *Ibid.*, pp. 207-36.

34 Mildred Aldrich, *A Hilltop on the Marne* (Boston: Houghton Mifflin, 1917); and *On the Edge of the War Zone* (Cambridge: Cambridge University Press, 1917).

35 Brinnin, *The Third Rose*, p. 216.

36 See Robert Bartlett Haas and Donald Clifford Gallup, *A Catalogue of the Published and Unpublished Writings of Gertrude Stein* (New Haven: Yale University Press, 1941), pp. 37-43, for a complete listing of Gertrude Stein's contributions to periodicals.

37 Gertrude Stein, "Vacation in Britany," *Little Review* 8 (Spring 1922):5-6.

38 Haas and Gallup, *A Catalogue of the Published and Unpublished Writings*, p. 49.

39 Quoted by permission of Calman A. Levin of the offices of Daniel C. Joseph, administrator of the estate of Gertrude Stein. This work is now available in *Reflections on the Atom Bomb. Volume I of the Previously Uncollected Writings of Gertrude Stein*, Robert Bartlett Haas, ed. (Los Angeles: Black Sparrow Press, 1974), pp. 77-78.

40 There is some confusion about the exact location to which Stein is referring in the title of this piece. The confusion has been created by the lack of uniformity in the spelling of the title. The *Little Review* published the piece under the spelling, "Vacation in Britany," however, Haas and Gallup refer to it as "Vacation in Brittany." Because Haas and Gallup's *A Catalogue of the Published and Unpublished Writings*, contains other errors in title names of Stein's

work (for example, it lists *Mrs. Reynolds* under the erroneous title *Mr. Reynolds*), the work cannot always be taken without question. I have used the title which was published in the *Little Review*, "Vacation in Britany," because although the locale in paragraph one of the piece certainly reminds one of Brittany with its seashore and white stone farmhouses, and "walls that scale," it is entirely possible that Gertrude Stein intentionally spelled it "Britany" rather than "Brittany" in order to utilize the suggestiveness of "bright-any" (which that spelling would imply). If that was Stein's intent, then, the spelling "Britany" would combine the suggestion of the locale of Brittany with the sun and whiteness suggested in "Britany." In view of Stein's whimsical humor, and delight in word play, this explanation of the spelling does not seem to me to be unreasonable.

41 Stein, "A Transatlantic Interview," p. 18.

42 Sutherland, *Gertrude Stein*, p. 75.

43 Gertrude Stein, "Made a Mile Away," *Transition* 8 (November 1927):155-65.

44 Haas and Gallup, *A Catalogue of the Published and Unpublished Writings*, p. 51.

45 Gertrude Stein, "Pictures," *Lectures in America* (New York: Random House, 1935), p. 78.

46 *Ibid.*, pp. 59-90.

47 Gertrude Stein, "J. H. Jane Heap," *Little Review* 12 (May 1929):9-10.

48 Haas and Gallup, *A Catalogue of the Published and Unpublished Writings*, p. 52.

49 Written in 1927; *Ibid.*, p. 52.

50 Brinnin, *The Third Rose*, p. 251.

51 The incident is recorded in Stein, *The Autobiography of Alice B. Toklas*, p. 271 as follows:

Jane Heap turned up one afternoon. The Little Review had

printed the Birthplace of Bonnes and the Valentine to Sherwood Anderson. Jane Heap sat down and we began to talk. She stayed to dinner and she stayed the evening and by dawn the little ford car Godiva which had been burning its lights all night waiting to be taken home could hardly start to take Jane home. Gertrude Stein then and always liked Jane Heap immensely, Margaret Anderson interested her much less.

52 Gertrude Stein, *Lucy Church Amiably* (Paris: Plain Edition, 1930).

53 Haas and Gallup, *A Catalogue of the Published and Unpublished Writings*, p. 52.

54 Richard Bridgman, *Gertrude Stein in Pieces* (New York: Oxford University Press, 1970), p. 189.

55 Stein, "Pictures," pp. 62-65.

56 Bridgman, *Gertrude Stein in Pieces*, pp. 189-90, suggests that this represents a defect in Stein's conception of the work. He writes:

As often happens with her privately generated projects Gertrude Stein started off enthusiastically, then lost momentum, until at last she was obliged to rely upon sheer eccentricity to carry her to a point that she could designate as the end.

However, Bridgman often presents assessments of Stein's work in axioms such as these, without, apparently, feeling that any support of his axiom is required.

57 Bridgman, *Gertrude Stein in Pieces*, p. 190. (Alice Toklas and Gertrude Stein were vacationing in Belley and in Bilignin at the time this work was written.)

58 This notion is discussed at some length by Lemaitre, *From Cubism to Surrealism*, p. 45. I have paraphrased it above. Lemaitre actually says of Mallarmé, "Just as a spark is more easily seen in the darkness, so the poetical effulgence of words will be more vividly apparent in the midst of dialectic obscurity."

59 Sutherland, *Gertrude Stein*, p. 138, has called this work a "pastoral romance."

60 Stein's three major critics are: Donald Sutherland, John Malcolm Brinnin, and Richard Bridgman. It is the two latter ones who suggest that Stein's identity with the woman Lucy Church is important. See Bridgman, *Gertrude Stein in Pieces*, p. 191: "The woman generally resembles Gertrude Stein at her best, relaxed and on vacation. . . . The notion of herself as a church accorded with the religious orientation of Gertrude Stein's recent thought." See also, Brinnin, *The Third Rose*, p. 295: "Her heroine, Lucy Church, is often unmistakably Gertrude Stein herself, so that the ultimate effect of the work is a sense of her mind continually thinking and recording its thoughts in the midst of a pastoral that is itself perpetually in motion."

61 Stein, "A Transatlantic Interview," p. 19.

The Later Years: 1932-1944

THE AUTOBIOGRAPHY
OF ALICE B. TOKLAS

As we have seen, during Stein's middle period the major thrust of her experimentation was with the nonrepresentational use of language. However, we noted that during those years she was also working to remove the spatial metaphor of time from her writing. Her novels and portraits did not contain temporally presented events in the lives of her characters. We noted further that the time which *was* present was the "liquid" time of duration.

During the years which we are about to examine, Gertrude Stein turned away from experiments with nonrepresentational language toward a much closer examination of time than she had attempted in any of her earlier works. That is not to say that she was no longer interested in the many dimensions of language that she had explored earlier. It is, rather, to suggest that she had already carried these experimentations to the point where she became interested in a new challenge, which was, as she wrote in "A Transatlantic Interview," the return to the narrative form in an attempt to conquer what she had called the "falsity of time." Discussing her return to the narrative she said,

> I found out that in the essence of narration is this problem of time. You have as a person writing, and all the really great narration has it, you have to denude yourself of time so that writing time does not exist. If time exists, your writing is ephemeral. You can have a historical time, but for you the time does not exist, and if you are writing about the present, the time element must cease to exist. I did it unconsciously in the *Autobiography of Alice Toklas*, but I did it consciously in *Everybody's Autobiography* and in the last thing *Wars I Have Seen*. In it I described something momentous happening under my eyes and I was able to do it without a great sense of time. There should not be a sense of time, but an existence suspended in time.[1]

The major thrust of Stein's interest in these later years then, is the challenge of the presentation of time. For her exploration of this interest she chose the two most challenging time genres there are: autobiography and history.

She began her return to the narrative form with *The Autobiography of Alice B. Toklas*.[2] This work represents a major departure from Stein's previous literary inclinations. The language is simple, accessible and straightforward; and, for the first time ever, she employs a narrator who is also a character in the work. With such dramatic differences from past works, it was inevitable that even Stein's authorship of the work would come into question.[3] However, to say that this work departs from previous Stein works is clearly not enough.

The fact is that Gertrude Stein wrote five autobiographical works during her career[4] and that at least the first three of them use different narrative voices, or aliases. The point is most important to the discussion of *The Autobiography of Alice B. Toklas.* But we will consider it in detail when we come to the third kind of narrative voice — the voice in *Everybody's Autobiography* — and there compare the three.

According to Stein, her authorship of the autobiography of Alice Toklas came about as a joke. Her recollection proves, however, that behind the joke lay a serious artistic experiment:

After the *Four Saints*[5] the portrait narration began, and I went back to the form of narration, and at that time I had a certain reputation, no success, but a certain reputation, and I was asked to write a biography, and I said 'No.' And then as a joke I began to write the *Autobiography of Alice Toklas,* and at that moment I had made a rather interesting discovery. A young French poet had begun to write, and I was asked to translate his poems, and there I made a rather startling discovery that other people's words are quite different from one's own, and that they can not be the result of your internal troubles as a writer. They have a totally different sense than when they are your own words. This solved for me the problem of Shakespeare's sonnets, which are so unlike any of his other work. These may have been his own idea, undoubtedly they were, but the words have none of the violence that exists in any of the poems, in any of the plays. They have a roughness and violence in their juxtapostion which the sonnets do not have, and this brought me to a great deal of illumination of narrative, because most narrative is based not about your opinions but upon someone else's.

Therefore narrative has a different concept than poetry or even exposition, because, you see, the narrative in itself is not what is in your mind but what is in somebody else's. Plays use it less, and so I did a tour de force with the *Autobiography of Alice Toklas,* and when I sent the first half to the agent, they sent back a telegram to see which one of us had written it! But still I had done what I saw, what you do in translation or in a narrative. I had recreated the point of view of somebody else.[6]

The Autobiography of Alice B. Toklas is often used as a source book for facts and attitudes which scholars attribute to Gertrude Stein. However, certain "facts" in that work are not true, and should not be taken as the literal truth of what was in Stein's mind, but rather "What is in somebody else's." This is an important point because it not only explains why some of the information in the *Autobiography* is not true, but also accounts for Stein's dramatic departures in the work, for the book is an attempt to see the world through the eyes of Alice Toklas, not those of Gertrude Stein.

The "autobiography" is divided into seven sections, organized, at first glance, chronologically. Alice Toklas is the first-person narrator of the work. However, both chronology and Alice Toklas are *manipulated*.

The manipulation of time is, of course, related to the manipulation of the narrator. We must separate them long enough to examine each closely, then put them back together again. At that time we will consider the ways in which this narrator, like the narrators in Stein's other autobiographical works, is an alias for Stein.

The seven sections of *The Autobiography of Alice B. Toklas* are entitled:

I. Before I Came to Paris
II. My Arrival in Paris
III. Gertrude Stein in Paris — 1903-1907
IV. Gertrude Stein Before She Came to Paris
V. 1907-1914
VI. The War
VII. After the War — 1919-1932

It is apparent that the work begins quite conventionally with the history of Toklas before she went abroad to live permanently. It will also be noticed, however, that her life previous to that time is given only four pages — the first twenty-eight years of her life are covered in four pages out of a total of three-hundred-and-ten.[7] The second chapter, in which Toklas meets Stein, covers only a few months but is given twenty-eight pages. An even more interesting fact is that Alice Toklas arrived in Paris in 1907, and she could not possibly have been the eye-witness first-person narrator of sections three and four, since they antedate sections one and two. In other words, the book is organized in the following sequence: 1877-1906[8]; 1907; 1903-1907; 1874-1903[9]; 1907-1914; 1914-1918; 1919-1932. The question is, why is the book so obviously out of sequence in sections three and four?

Obviously the central figure in the book is to be Stein, and not the narrator, Toklas.[10] The first section, as briefly as it treats the early years of Toklas, concludes with her meeting Gertrude Stein and declaring her to be one of the three "geniuses" she has ever met (6). The second section shows the artistic life Gertrude Stein and her brother Leo led in Paris. The time of this chapter is 1907, and it is given over completely to Alice Toklas's impressions of the artistic scene in Paris during that year. It begins with Gertrude Stein's achievements, which are immediately related to the other important events in Paris at that time. Following is the first paragraph of the chapter. Notice how fundamentally Gertrude Stein is woven into the scene by the narrator.

This was the year 1907. Gertrude Stein was just seeing through

127

the press Three Lives which she was having privately printed, and she was deep in The Making of Americans, her thousand page book. Picasso had just finished his portrait of her which nobody at that time liked except the painter and the painted and which is now so famous, and he had just begun his strange complicated picture of three women, Matisse had just finished his Bonheur de Vivre, his first big composition which gave him the name of fauve or a zoo. It was the moment Max Jacob has since called the heroic age of cubism. I remember not long ago hearing Picasso and Gertrude Stein talking about various things that had happened at that time, one of them said but all that could not have happened in that one year, oh said the other, my dear you forget we were young then and we did a great deal in a year. (7)

The above paragraph is a good indication of the general thrust of the rest of the chapter. The narrator, having established the importance of Gertrude Stein in the artistic scene of 1907, is then seen about to enter the famous Stein household for dinner. Through the remainder of the chapter the reader "sees" these famous friends of the Steins, some of whom also appear at the dinner party, and some of whom come in later for one of the famous Stein Saturday evenings. Primarily through anecdote and occasional dialogue, these famous people are pictured as always grouped around Gertrude Stein as the central figure of importance. (The methods employed by the narrator in the presentation of these famous figures will be covered later, during the discussion of the narrator as such.) Notice here that the great importance of Gertrude Stein to this artistic scene is well set in the mind of the reader before any earlier view of Stein is presented. It is as if the narrator must make sure that the reader appreciates Stein's importance first, before being given any of the facts of her early life. This is the primary accomplishment of, and reason for, the manipulation of chronology in these chapters.

Another glance at the table of contents will bear out this idea. The second chapter takes place during 1907, and attempts to establish Gertrude Stein as an important figure during that important year. Having established this, primarily through portraying the famous figures who were intimates of the Steins, the narrator could well have gone back to the conventional time method, beginning with the birth of Gertrude Stein and continuing to the present. But, this is not the method of the narrator. She chooses to begin with the arrival of Gertrude Stein in Paris, and her movement into the artistic scene just described in chapter two. Not until she has demonstrated the solidarity of Gertrude Stein's "rightful" place among the artists of Paris of 1907 does the narrator choose to go farther back in Stein's life, to the beginning.

Chapter three then, "Gertrude Stein in Paris — 1903-1907," is filled with anecdotes about the artists Leo and Gertrude Stein knew before 1907 — primarily Cézanne. Many stories are told about Leo and Gertrude Stein as important art collectors, and, incidentally, how their patronage aided many unknown painters who were starving. It can be seen from even this brief adumbration of the chapter that Gertrude Stein emerges with an increasingly important place in the artistic world with which the book is concerned.

With this position assured in both chapters two and three, the narrator is then certain that the reader will be deeply interested in Gertrude Stein's childhood. And so we see the next chapter, "Gertrude Stein Before She

129

Came to Paris," following the other two, even though it is out of order chronologically.

There is a second kind of time, quite apart from the over-all chronological organization, in this work — the kind of time Stein was referring to when she said, "There should not be a sense of time, but an existence suspended in time." It is in this concept that the importance of the narrator lies.

Bear in mind that the narrator of this work is also a character in it, and as such she bears an interesting relationship to a character such as Marlow, the narrator of *Heart of Darkness.* This point has not been made by any other investigator, and perhaps should not be insisted upon very seriously. However, the view the reader gets of Kurtz in *Heart of Darkness* is wholly contingent upon both the personality of Marlow and the accidents of time which make certain bits of information possible to Marlow. The real similarities between the two narrators are those which allow their creators to dispense with the conventional time lines in portraying the true central characters (Stein in *The Autobiography of Alice B. Toklas,* and Kurtz in *Heart of Darkness*) in favor of those highly selected incidents in the lives of the central characters which function to spotlight *only what the author wishes to spotlight.* With this kind of narrator, the author is no longer tyrannized by the demands of chronology. For, after all, "if time exists, your writing is ephemeral," as Stein said in "A Transatlantic Interview"(20).

Another advantage of a first-person narrator in any kind of work is that of the "veil of reality"[11] which the first person creates. In this case, Alice Toklas as narrator can bring about the "lionization" of Stein in a way that Stein could never have accomplished with the same degree of believability had the work been written with herself as narrator. Consider the credibility of the following passage, as seen through the eyes of Alice Toklas rather than through Stein's own eyes.

> Mrs. [Michael] Stein brought with her three little Matisse paintings, the first modern things to cross the Atlantic. I made her acquaintance at this time of general upset and she showed them to me, she also told me many stories of her life in Paris. Gradually I told my father that perhaps I would leave San Francisco. He was not disturbed by this, after all there was at that time a great deal of going and coming and there were many friends of mine going. Within a year I also had gone and I had come to Paris. There I went to see Mrs. Stein who had in the meantime returned to Paris, and there at her house I met Gertrude Stein. I was impressed by the coral brooch she wore and by her voice. I may say that only three times in my life have I met a genius and each time a bell within me rang and I was not mistaken, and I may say in each case it was before there was any general recognition of the quality of genius in them. The three geniuses of whom I wish to speak are Gertrude Stein, Pablo Picasso and Alfred Whitehead. [5-6]

The "veil of reality" mentioned above can be seen at work here. The narrator's voice is low-keyed and apparently objective. She had described herself, previous to the above passage thus: "I myself have had no liking for violence and have always enjoyed the pleasures of needlework and gardening. I am fond of paintings, furniture, tapestry, houses and flowers even vegetables and fruit-trees. I like a view but I like to sit with my back turned to it" (3). This is a picture of a quiet, unassuming, normal, trustworthy, amusing voice that the reader has little difficulty believing in. Therefore, when this narrator calls Stein a "genius" the reader does not face the problem of credibility he faces when Gertrude Stein calls herself one — which she has done in several other works.

It is one of Stein's accomplishments with this first-person narrator that she does not allow its usual disadvantages — that the eyewitness is limited to what he could have credibly witnessed himself — to restrain her. She simply ignores that conventional limitation and permits an eyewitness who was not there to relate one-fourth of the material.

The following incident, related by Toklas, occurs in the chapter, "Gertrude Stein in Paris — 1903-1907." Toklas could not possibly have been present during this incident, but Stein, the author, handles Toklas's narration of it so smoothly that the reader is not even aware of the fact until the second or third reading of the book. The incident covers several pages and cannot be quoted in full, but a selection from it follows. Keep in mind that the entire incident took place some four years before Toklas met Stein.

> During Gertrude Stein's last two years at the Medical School, Johns Hopkins, Baltimore, 1900-1903, her brother was living in Florence. There he heard of a painter named Cézanne and saw paintings by him. . . . When he and his sister made their home in Paris the following year they went to Vollard's the only picture dealer who had Cézannes for sale, to look at them.
>
> Vollard was a huge dark man who lisped a little. . . . The first visit to Vollard has left an indelible impression on Gertrude Stein. It was an incredible place. It did not look like a picture gallery. Inside there were a couple of canvases turned to the wall, in one corner was a small pile of big and little canvases thrown pell mell on top of one another, in the centre of the room stood a huge man glooming. This was Vollard cheerful. When he was really cheerless he put his huge frame against the glass door that led to the street, his arms above his head, his hands

on each upper corner of the portal and gloomed darkly into the
street. Nobody thought then of trying to come in.
They asked to see Cézannes. He looked less gloomy and
became quite polite. . . .[35-36]

The passage begins with the sort of factual information
that anyone could have known about Gertrude and Leo
Stein, and it is probable that Toklas, as the narrator,
could have known it. However, notice the smoothness
of the transition to information that Toklas was highly
unlikely to have known in just such detail: "Vollard
was a huge dark man. . . ." Of course, Toklas could
have known he was a huge dark man, but the transition
and what follows imply that the description of him is
related to *that* day when "they went to Vollard's." Since
they went to Vollard's that day some four years before
Toklas met them, the visit which "left such an indelible
impression on Gertrude Stein's mind," is miraculously
recreated in the following paragraph (considering that
the narrator wasn't even there). The details involving
the description of Vollard and his gallery are too full of
specifics to have been written by someone who had not
been present. It may be that the reader does not realize
this point on first reading since Stein has so cleverly
disguised the fact by creating a detailed pictorial
description which so involves the reader that he fails to
see that this narrator could not have been present at
this exact time and in this exact place.

The remainder of the incident is even less believable
because it reports extended dialogue between the
characters. The dialogue is necessary to the humor of
the incident, as is the distance created by the narrator,
and Stein does not hesitate to present it all through the
eyes and ears of this narrator.

133

They told Monsieur Vollard they wanted to see some Cézanne landscapes. . . . Oh yes, said Vollard looking quite cheerful and he began moving about the room, finally he disappeared behind a partition in the back and was heard heavily mounting the steps. After a quite long wait he came down again and had in his hand a tiny picture of an apple with most of the canvas unpainted. They all looked at this thoroughly, then they said, yes but you see what we wanted to see was a landscape. Ah yes, sighed Vollard and he looked even more cheerful, after a moment he again disappeared and this time came back with a painting of a back, it was a beautiful painting there is no doubt about that but the brother and sister were not yet up to a full appreciation of Cézanne nudes and so they returned to the attack. They wanted to see a landscape. This time after even a longer wait he came back with a very large canvas and a very little fragment of a landscape painted on it. Yes that was it, they said, a landscape but what they wanted was a smaller canvas but one all covered. They said, they thought they would like to see one like that. By this time the early winter evening of Paris was closing in and just at this moment a very aged charwoman came down the same back stairs . . . and quietly went out of the door, after a moment another old charwoman came down the same stairs . . . and went quietly out of the door. Gertrude Stein began to laugh and said to her brother, it is all nonsense, there is no Cézanne. Vollard goes upstairs and tells these old women what to paint and he does not understand us and they do not understand him and they paint something and he brings it down and it is a Cézanne. They both began to laugh uncontrollably. [37-38]

Robert Haas has said that Gertrude Stein became "her own Boswell,"[12] in this work. As can be seen from the passage just quoted, his remark has some justification — "some" with a firm reservation. The details and the dialogue of an incident which the narrator, Toklas, could not possibly know, and which, therefore, have been recreated by one of the actual eyewitnesses — the author — are the important factors. Gertrude Stein did not become her own Boswell; she went Samuel Johnson one better by *creating* her own Boswell. Alice Toklas is a *fictional* character in *The Autobiography of Alice B. Toklas*. No one has ever suggested that this work bears closer resemblance to a novel than it does to an "autobiography," and perhaps we should not insist upon that idea. But from the passage just quoted one can see that the personality of Gertrude Stein is illuminated in the telling of this incident in a way which would have been impossible in a conventional autobiography. The figure emerges slowly, cumulatively through the presentation of her as a character in a story. She is seen through other people's eyes, not her own, but Stein retains the advantage of selecting her own materials. So we may say that she has "created" Alice Toklas, through means not given to Samuel Johnson — who had no hand in the creation of Boswell.

It was an original premise of this argument that the "autobiography" was a major departure from Gertrude Stein's previous works. Indeed, there is a sense in which it may be considered a departure from anything ever written. (To my knowledge, no author has ever attempted a self-portrait seen through the eyes of another living person.) Be that as it may, this entire matter gives rise to consideration of another departure: throughout her career Stein wrote autobiographical materials with a narrative "mask." In "Two: Gertrude Stein and Her Brother" the narrator was the third person, whose mask was akin to that of the *histor*. Gertrude Stein presented herself in the third person.

The narrator in *The Autobiography of Alice B. Toklas* is another mask — another narrator who is the "not me"

— Gertrude Stein again presents herself in the third person. Although it is fairly clear that there were many advantages in the use of the third-person technique in both works, the question still persists: why these narrative masks? We confront this question, and attempt to deal with it in yet another autobiographical work.

EVERYBODY'S AUTOBIOGRAPHY

The Autobiography of Alice B. Toklas was a "spectacular best seller."[13] Largely because of its success, Gertrude Stein was induced to return to the United States in 1935, after an absence of thirty years, for an extended lecture tour. John Malcolm Brinnin describes the acclaim which came to Gertrude Stein as a result of the popularity of the work. He describes *The Autobiography of Alice B. Toklas* as "... the best seller, which inevitably brought her into the lecture halls of the United States and imposed upon her name celebrity of such proportions that her eminence on the American scene was for a time shared only by gangsters, baseball players and movie stars" (308).

Everybody's Autobiography[14] covers the events of that lecture tour, for the most part, and the inevitable memories of her youth in America which the return after so long a time would naturally recall to her mind. Gertrude Stein saw her triumphant return to America as not solely the result of the success of the *Autobiography*. She wrote:

> [Albert] Harcourt was very surprised when I said to him on first meeting him in New York remember this extraordinary welcome that I am having does not come from the books of mine that they do understand like the Autobiography but the books of mine that they do not understand and he called his

partner and said listen to what she says and perhaps after all she is right.[15]

At least three conclusions may be reached in analyzing this passage. First, and most obvious, is that although *Everybody's Autobiography* is her third autobiographical work, it is the first one using a first-person narrator whose identity is the same as the author's. Second, the contents of the passage show that the narrator is concerned with her identity as an entity — she is focusing on her entire career as a writer and not alone on the success of *The Autobiography of Alice B. Toklas*. Third, and perhaps not quite so obvious, the idiosyncratic use of punctuation in the passage creates a durational voice in the narration. These three points will be examined one at a time.

The narrator of the first obviously autobiographical work Stein wrote, "Two: Gertrude Stein and Her Brother," utilized a third-person narrator even though the work was autobiographical. The same is true in *The Autobiography of Alice B. Toklas* — the work is *about* Gertrude Stein *by* Gertrude Stein, although seen through the eyes of another. Clearly the author of these works disguises herself with an identity — or a mask — of the "not me." There is an interesting parallel in *Everybody's Autobiography*. Even the first-person narrator of this work is disguised.

Writing of her problems with autobiography as a genre in *Everybody's Autobiography*, Stein said:

... identity is funny being yourself is funny as you are never yourself to yourself except as you remember yourself and then of course you do not believe yourself. That is really the trouble with an autobiography you do not of course you do not really believe yourself why should you, you know so well so very well that it is not yourself, it could not be yourself because you cannot remember right and if you do remember right it does not sound right and of course it does not sound right because it is not right. You are of course never yourself . . . . [68]

A comparison of the three narrative techniques used in the three autobiographical works demonstrates that Stein attempted to handle the mercurial aspects of identity in autobiography in three dissimilar ways. All three examples deal with her relationship with her brother Leo.

In the following example from "Two," the narrator is obviously trying to treat both characters "objectively," and at the same time to preserve the mystery of the problem of identity, which make necessary the choices, on the one hand, of the third-person narrator, and on the other, of the fluid participial form:

> He being one and needing being one feeling that he was creating being living was needing that sound sounding was coming out of him. She being one and needing being feeling that being living she was creating was needing that sound sounding was coming out of her. [39]

Compare the picture of Leo Stein as seen through the eyes of Alice Toklas in *The Autobiography of Alice B. Toklas.* (It is an essential part of this discussion that Alice Toklas could not possibly have witnessed the following event. Therefore, even though Stein said she had created the point of view of someone else in this work, what follows was not witnessed by Alice Toklas at all, it having occurred two years before Toklas met Stein.)

> That evening Gertrude Stein's brother took out portfolio after portfolio of japanese prints to show Picasso, Gertrude Stein's brother was fond of japanese prints. Picasso solemnly and obe-

diently looked at print after print and listened to the descriptions. He said under his breath to Gertrude Stein, he is very nice, your brother, but like all americans . . . he shows you japanese prints. . . . I don't care for it. As I say Gertrude Stein and Pablo Picasso immediately understood each other. [56]

The important point here is that the anecdote is presented by the narrator in such a way as to make it appear that there were four people present when the event happened — Leo, Gertrude, Pablo, and Alice. In fact, there were only the first three. There is every indication that the picture of Leo Stein as an unoriginal bore, very much out of step with the two geniuses in the room that night, is not the conclusion of the objective narrator, but rather the result of an Alice Toklas mask which Gertrude Stein was wearing when she wrote it.

It is of surpassing interest to note that whenever Gertrude Stein talks about her relationship with her brother Leo in *Everybody's Autobiography* she uses some device to provide distance.[16] On one page alone (72), the narrator recalls something Alice Toklas said about Leo, then something their Uncle Ephraim said about him, followed by something Alfred Stieglitz said. Gertrude Stein always seems to need some intermediary when referring to her relationship with Leo. Even when the narrator speaks of the genuinely deep feelings between Gertrude and Leo, she finds it useful to introduce the matter by saying that she is relating something she told to another person (William Seabrook) one night at dinner (68). It is as if even in her autobiography, with herself as first-person narrator, she still chooses not to approach the subject of her relationship with Leo "head-on." The following is a selection from the "story" she told to Seabrook.

> That is the way [Leo] felt about it and it was a natural thing, because he understood everything and if you understand everything and besides that are leading and besides that do do what you do there is no reason why it should not be creating, and that is he was that and had always been and I had not been that but I had been it enough to be following, now why should it come to be that it should be something else now just why should it. Well well just why should it. The only thing about it was that it was I who was the genius. . . . [77]

The narrator, in this passage, is attempting to be as objective about Leo Stein as the narrator of "Two" had tried to be. There is a parallel between the stringing together of slightly differing participles in "Two," and the fluidity created by the lack of punctuation in the passage cited above.[17] In both cases the form itself gives a feeling of distance, since it gives the impression that the narrator is honestly trying to capture the truth of the event. When Gertrude Stein wrote that the problem with autobiographical materials is that they never seem "right" to the author, she was apparently trying to explain why she had used so many different approaches to her own autobiographical works.

It is not enough to suggest that Stein's experimentation with the narrative voice in her autobiographical work was of psychological origin alone. The psychological explanation is, of course, the most commonly offered and, perhaps, the most plausible one. But it is also well to remember that a disappearing autobiographical personality might be still another facet of the Stein who felt impelled to purge ordinary fictional language of its references to narrative persona.

Everybody's Autobiography includes much material

not concerned directly with psychologically oriented matters. It offers many examples of Stein's stylistic experimentation with the release of the narrative voice. Shortly after she had written *The Autobiography of Alice B. Toklas,* Gertrude Stein wrote an article for *Vanity Fair* (September, 1934),[18] in which she discussed her reactions to the success of that work. After some consideration of the ways in which success can make a writer "sterile" (35), she continues by telling what she is doing now that the *Autobiography* is behind her. The section is illuminating because it points ahead to the writing of *Everybody's Autobiography:*

> I write the way I used to write in the Making of Americans, I wander around. I come home and write. . . . I have come back to write the way I used to write and this is because now everything that is happening is once more happening inside, there is no use in the outside, if you see the outside you see just what you look at and that is no longer interesting, everybody says so or at least everybody acts so and they are right because now there is no use in looking at anything. If it is going to change it is of no interest and if it is not going to change it is of no interest and so what is the use of looking, everything you see is what nobody looks at and so just as so long ago everything went on inside now everything goes on inside. . . .
> And so the time comes when I can tell the history of my life. [65]

The history of Gertrude Stein's life begins "Alice B. Toklas did hers and now anybody will do theirs." It is a very interesting dodge by the narrator since obviously Alice Toklas did *not* do hers, and who is *anybody?* Of course the narrator soon switches to the first person but the initial statement serves to place some distance between the narrator and the author all the way through the work. Donald Sutherland says that this

141

book is filled with "endless talk about herself and her writing and her opinions and the little incidents that happened to her. . . ."[19] And he makes the very interesting judgment that the endless talk about herself somehow results, contrary to expectation, in the creation of an aesthetic distance, which seems "objective" (153) to the reader. The feeling is heightened by the fluidity of run-on sentences.

Illustrative of this idea is a portion of *Everybody's Autobiography* which is not concerned with the relationship between Leo and Gertrude Stein. The excerpt concerns the meeting, and subsequent happenings, of Gertrude Stein with Robert Hutchins and Mortimer Adler in Chicago during Stein's lecture there. Hutchins was then president of the University of Chicago, and both he and Adler were famed educators.

> We went to dinner it was a good dinner. We were at dinner but Hutchins the president of Chicago University was not there later he came in with Mortimer Adler.
> Hutchins was tired and we all sat down again together and then he began talking about what he had been doing. He and Adler were having special classes and in them they were talking over all the ideas that had been important in the world's history. Every week they took a new idea and the man who had written it and the class read it and then they had a conversation about it.
> What are the ideas that are important I asked him. Here said he is the list of them I took the list and looked it over. Ah I said I notice that none of the books read at any time by them was originally written in English, was that intentional I asked him. No he said but in English there have really been no ideas expressed. Then I gather that to you there are no ideas which are not socio-logical or government ideas. Well are they [sic] he said, well yes I said. . . . [206]

What is so striking about this narrator is the

simplicity of the language and of the sentence structure. The distinguished educators are shredded by simple words and run-on sentences. That Hutchins and Adler (or indeed any one in the world) could be "talking over *all* the ideas that had been important in the world's history" (one a week), immediately establishes the two men as outrageously arrogant, although the narrator does not *say* that. It is not necessary to say it since, in the repetition of the undercutting pronoun "it" in the next sentence, the narrator underlines their pomposity without having to spell it out. "Each week they took a new idea and the man who had written it and the class read it and then they had a conversation about it." By the time the reader has encountered "it" for the third time, the referent has been pulverized.

The narrator then asks the simple, obvious, question: What are the ideas that are important? The educator simply reaches into his pocket for them, making the educator appear outrageously facile to the reader. But, again, the narrator does not draw that conclusion. She simply correlates the tabulation of great ideas with a list — suggesting a grocery list — always carried around in the educator's pocket.

The same method is seen in the disarming simplicity of the narrator's questions and answers. "Ah I said I notice that none of the books read at any time by them was originally written in English . . . ." Naturally the narrator, writing for an English-speaking audience, has every reader on her side with this question. Every one awaits the great man's answer. It is, ". . . in English there have been no great ideas expressed." The narrator has finished the educator, or, more to the point, the narrator has allowed the educator to finish himself, since it is the narrator's apparent objectivity which accomplished the destruction. Nowhere does the narrator *say* that Hutchins struck her as pompous. She simply runs all his great ideas together, with little punctuation, balancing the apparent simplicity of the language, created by the run-on sentences, against the weight of the ideas expressed by Hutchins. The attempt to balance these two opposites creates an ironic gap into which the famed educator falls.

Subsequent to the meeting at dinner, Hutchins and Adler invite Gertrude Stein to conduct a session of their class. The implication suggested by the narrator is that they hope Stein will make a fool of herself. Stein accepts the invitation and the narrator continues,

> I had gotten used to lecturing and did not think about that as a thing but here I was to be teaching and anything is a funny feeling and that was.
>
> So we all sat around a long table and Hutchins and Adler and I presiding, at least we were not to be but there we were as if we were, well anyway I began talking.
>
> I began to talk and they not Hutchins and Adler but the others began to talk and pretty soon we were all talking about epic poetry and what it was it was exciting we found out a good deal . . . in epic poetry you can have an epic because the death of the man meant the end of everything and now nothing is ending by the death of any one because something is already happening. Well we all came out and they liked it and I liked it and Hutchins said to me as he and I were walking, you did make them all talk more than we can make them and a number of them talked who never talked before and it was very nice of him to say it and he added and if you will come back I will be glad to have you do some teaching and I said I would . . . and then I said you see why they talk to me is that I am like them I do not know the answer, you say you do not know but you do know if

you did not know the answer you could not spend your life in teaching but I I really do not know, I really do not, I do not even know whether there is a question let alone having an answer for a question.[20] To me when a thing is really interesting it is when there is no question and no answer, if there is then already the subject is not interesting and it is so, that is the reason that anything for which there is a solution is not interesting, that is the trouble with governments and Utopias and teaching, the things not that can be learnt but that can be taught are not interesting. Well anyway we went away. [212-13]

Again the narrator's voice, the simplicity of the vocabulary, and the almost conversational tone created by the careful absence of punctuation, is a mask in itself.[21] The sense of time in the passage is immediate, as indeed it is in the entire book. But careful examination of a passage such as this one reveals that the simplicity, and what appears to be a disarming objectivity are really narrative devices made successful by the very fluidity which the absence of punctuation creates. It could also be called a durational voice. That is, when writing appears to be continuous — without interruptions of punctuation in the time-sense of the reader — the result is that the narrator appears to be conversing with the reader. This in itself creates an appearance of "truth" in the narrator.

Nowhere is this more evident than in the part of the passage just cited in which Stein's comments to Hutchins are given. The narrator has run all of Hutchins's "great ideas" together with little punctuation, thereby making them appear weaker than they might otherwise have seemed. Stein's own comments are presented with very careful punctuation designed to retain the durational voice through infrequent use of the period, but also to highlight the important thoughts through more frequent use of the comma than was accorded Hutchins. This is not meant to imply that the technique is unfair to Hutchins. It is merely a description of the narrative technique Stein had finally created — a first-person narrator capable of reflecting her image of herself credibly.[22] *Everybody's Autobiography*, primarily because of this narrative technique, offers a fascinating internal glimpse of Gertrude Stein. As Bridgman has said,

> It is understandable that in her own day, with stories about Gertrude Stein having filled the newspapers and magazines for several years with the impression that she was a diverting eccentric, the book should have been taken as a casual production, conceived for profit and exhibiting an egoism so inflated that it could not distinguish the line between prattle and ideas meriting public attention. Today, though, it is clear that *Everybody's Autobiography* is one of her major successes. In it Gertrude Stein took up the most desperate problems she was then suffering from and managed to convey them without diminishing their complexity. With her unguarded style she produced moments of wit and illumination in the pedestrian ruck of existence. . . . There are unappreciated depths to this book. . . . [284]

Another interesting point about this work concerns her next book, *Ida*. During her lecture tour, Gertrude Stein was constantly bombarded by questions from newsmen and critics concerning the "obscurity" of her writings. On the lecture tour she was haunted (as she had been all of her writing career) by people asking why she wrote "like that." In *Everybody's Autobiography* she recalls one such incident:

> We went to Berkeley and they had invited me I think it was the Phi Beta Kappa to lunch, and during the lunch there were a lot of them there everybody asked a question not everybody but a

good many, they thought I answered them very well the only
thing I remember is their asking why I do not write as I talk and
I said to them if they had invited Keats to lunch and they asked
him an ordinary question would they expect him to answer
with the Ode to the Nightingale. [291-92]

The point that Stein makes with this delightful rejoinder is that the author, when writing, is a separate
person, with problems of communication different
from those of the author when he is not writing. The
narrative voice in any author's work, according to
Stein, is the reflection of whatever interest that writer
has currently in focus. Indeed, the major premise of
this whole study has been that Stein's narrative voice
did change every time her interests as a writer
changed. Therefore her rejoinder to the Phi Beta Kappa
group expressed her dismay that her critics so often expected her narrative voice to "sound like her," when
her narrative voices were meant to deal with whatever
problems in communication she was dealing with at
any given time. She takes up the problem again in *Ida*.

IDA

Everybody's Autobiography (not *The Autobiography of
Alice B. Toklas*) is an important source book for many of
Gertrude Stein's emotional and intellectual positions.
One was her concern with what she saw as the loss of
her identity due to the enormous publicity resulting
from the success of *The Autobiography of Alice B. Toklas*.
It is a recurring theme in the years that followed.

Ida[23] is the fictionalization of Stein's fear that publicity creates the personality of the publicized person. In
the article she wrote for *Vanity Fair*, she spoke of the
personal effects of such publicity.

147

> What happened to me was this. When the success began and it was a success I got lost completely lost. You know the nursery rhyme, I am I because my little dog knows me. Well you see I did not know myself, I lost my personality. It has always been completely included in myself my personality as any personality naturally is, and here all of a sudden, I was not just I because so many people did know me. It was just the opposite of I am I because my little dog knows me. So many people knowing me I was I no longer. . . . [35]

Keeping in mind that Stein wrote the *Vanity Fair* article the year before her lecture tour of America (which was to bring her even more publicity) and that in any case the problem of identity had always been one of her central concerns, it is not surprising that her problems with publicity versus identity would be intensified. In fact, she recalls the nursery rhyme mentioned above several times in *Everybody's Autobiography*. At one point she wrote: "Settled down in Bilignin[24] I became worried about identity and remembered the Mother Goose, I am I because my little dog knows me and I was not sure but that that only proved the dog was he and not that I was I" (297).

When Gertrude Stein had finished the writing of *Everybody's Autobiography*, she apparently still had not resolved the worry about whether she was the Gertrude Stein she had known all those years or the Gertrude Stein the public had created.[25] She set about writing *Ida* immediately.

About this interesting little work which she subtitled, "A Novel," she wrote,

> . . . the novel as a form has not been successful in the Twentieth Century . . . biographies have been more successful that novels. This is due in part to this enormous publicity business. The Duchess of Windsor was a more real person to the public and

while the divorce was going on was a more actual person than anyone could create. In the Nineteenth Century no one was played up like that, like the Lindbergh kidnapping really roused people's feelings. Then Eleanor Roosevelt is an actuality more than any character in the Twentieth Century novel ever achieved.

. . . That makes the novel scheme quite out of the question. One falls back on the thing like I did in *Ida,* where you try to handle a more or less satirical picture within the individual. No individual that you can conceive can hold their own beside life.[26]

The world of the novel *Ida* is a dream world,[27] inhabited by dream characters and dream situations. The locale of the work is the entire breadth of the United States — just as Stein's lecture tour had been two years previously. Ida marries four times without any reference to divorce. In essence, the plot, the settings, and the characters are all of the internal world of the human mind — with the thematic thread of how anyone knows his own identity running through it.

Stein referred to the work as "satirical." It is, and it is not. The narrator is satirical, and Ida's quest for identity is satirically handled. But neither the ending of the work, nor the deep concern with its theme, and its ultimately optimistic resolution, are genuinely satirical. The book ends with the word, "Yes." However, the narrator of this work is the most interesting aspect of it, and shows Stein in one of her best efforts.

If the world of *Ida* is a dream world (it even has talking spiders, goldfish and cuckoos), then the narrator is the very stuff that dreams are made on. He is the kind of third-person narrator Stein had mastered in *Three Lives.* The narrator, by echoing the speech rhythms and patterns of the characters, appears to blend into the book. While he is also "objective" in the sense that he never comments on any of the action, the similarities with earlier narrative techniques end there. The narrator of *Ida* is a very special narrator indeed.

The beginning of the book illustrates the point.

> There was a baby born named Ida. Its mother held it with her hands to keep Ida from being born but when the time came Ida came. And as Ida came, with her came her twin, so there was Ida-Ida. [7]

Two things are immediately noteworthy. The first is that anyone who has ever witnessed the birth of a child, as Stein had in her medical school experience, knows what is inherent in the idea that "the mother held it with her hands to keep it from being born." Almost all of the hopelessness and futility that a human gesture is capable of is in that sentence. This must be a dream then, because most women in labor — far from trying to prevent the birth — would do anything to get it over with. (And what would she do with the baby were she successful in preventing the birth?) The second noteworthy element in the opening statement is not obvious at first reading. The narrator is not reporting a literal fact when he says "with her came her twin." Ida is a single birth. The reference to Ida-Ida is a symbolic one: for Ida's identity is not clear from the moment she is born. The fact is that it is Ida who creates the twin Ida-Ida (later in the work), because she desperately wants a new identity. So, from the beginning, the narrator indicates that the world of this novel is very peculiar, and that he is to be an integral part of its peculiarities.

Shortly after Ida's birth, her parents ". . . went off on a trip and never came back" (8). Ida then begins her long dream association of living with strangers who do not know her. Her world is peopled with threatening strangers, mostly men, who appear and disappear with the unexplained frequency of a half dream, half fairy tale. Ida is living with a great aunt when the following two incidents happen to her:

> She was very young and as she had nothing to do she walked as if she was tall as tall as any one. Once she was lost that is to say a man followed her and that frightened her so that she was crying just as if she had been lost. In a little while that is some time after it was a comfort to her that this thing had happened to her. . . .
>
> One day it was not Tuesday, two people came to see her great-aunt. They came in very carefully. They did not come in together. First one came and then the other one. One of them had some orange blossoms in her hand. That made Ida feel funny. Who were they? She did not know and she did not like to follow them in. A third came along, this one was a man and he had orange blossoms in his hat brim. He took off his hat and he said to himself here I am, I wish to speak to myself. Here I am. [8-9]

The narrator of this passage is totally unreliable. That is part of the sheer fun of the whole book. He never gets time concepts right, "In a little while that is some time after." Nor can he be counted on for numerical concepts. He says that two people came to see Ida's great aunt and then explains what the first and the third did.

Shortly after this episode, Ida loses her great aunt and goes to live with her grandfather. Here she acquires a dog, named Love, who had been born blind, and obviously is intended to show Ida in search of affection. She is very lonesome and decides to have a twin.

> One day, it was before or after she made up her mind to be a

151

twin, she joined a walking marathon.[28] She kept on moving, sleeping or walking, she kept on slowly moving. This was one of the funny things that happened to her. Then she lived outside of a city, she was eighteen then, she decided that she had had enough of only being one and she told her dog Love that she was going to be two she was going to be a twin. And this did then happen.

Ida often wrote letters to herself that is to say she wrote to her twin. [18]

The letter which follows is a narrative device. Stein does not wish to show Ida, ever, internally. We never get into Ida's mind. Instead, when Stein wishes to show something that is in Ida's mind, we are offered such thoughts in letter form. It is perhaps fair to say that to show anyone's mind internally would be to lose some of the distance necessary to the dream world of this work. The letter gives us Ida's first real verbalization of her search for identity.

Dear Ida my twin,

Here I am sitting not alone because I have dear Love with me, and I speak to him and he speaks to me, but here I am all alone and I am thinking of you Ida my dear twin. Are you beautiful as beautiful as I am dear twin Ida, are you, and if you are perhaps I am not. I can not go away Ida, I am here always, if not here then somewhere, but just now I am here, I am like that, but you dear Ida you are not, you are not here, if you were I could not write to you. Do you know what I think Ida, I think that you could be a queen of beauty, one of the ones they elect when everybody has a vote. They are elected and they go everywhere and everybody looks at them and everybody sees them. Dear Ida oh dear Ida do do be one. Do not let them know you have any name but Ida and I know Ida will win, Ida Ida Ida,

from your twin
Ida.
[18-19]

Ida wins the beauty contest and is forever called Winnie because she has won it.

The letter, and the fact that by winning she loses her identity, can be related to Gertrude Stein's concern with her own "lost personality" through the publicity of success. (Maybe your little dog will know you under these circumstances and maybe he won't.) When Ida says "are you as beautiful as I am, and if you are perhaps I am not," she is surely referring to the double identity that results from a great deal of publicity — one's idea of oneself compared with the public idea of that identity. And when the public identity takes over, is the "private" aspect of that identity lost?

It is important in this context to mention that words such as "here," "there," "when," and "then," had a special significance for Stein. Ida's unique, wandering existence in this work is summed up by the narrator as, "She lives where she is not" (63). An anecdote from Alice Toklas's memoirs illuminates Stein's interests in these concepts:

> Gertrude at this time was absorbed in the story of Sylvia Pankhurst, who had been arrested for her too active interest in securing the vote for women. Miss Pankhurst was told that she must appear at the time her trial would take place. She said, I will be there. She was not. When the trial took place she was somewhere else. She said, That place was where *there* was. [62-63]

(Gertrude Stein has forever immortalized Oakland, California, where she grew up, in *Everybody's Autobiography* by saying that the only thing wrong with it is that "there is no there there" [289].)

The other major characters in *Ida*, for the most part the men she marries, fare no better than Ida does in terms of recognizable identity. The first three are men whose profession requires that they wear some kind of uniform — army officers, and policemen. When they appear in the story we see them out of uniform, as does Ida, and she marries each of them never knowing that they usually wore uniforms; that is, she never knew their real identity.

Finally, Ida meets and marries Andrew, and reaches some kind of "rest" from her search. "Ida returned more and more to be Ida. She even said she was Ida" (146). The final note of the book is almost one of living happily ever after: "she dresses in another hat and she dresses in another dress and Andrew is in, and they go in and that is where they are. They are there. Thank them. Yes" (154).

We can see that the relationship which emerges at the end of this work is very much like that between the principal characters in Stein's last novel, *Mrs. Reynolds*, to be treated next. But, since the narrative technique of *Ida* remains in a class by itself in Stein's corpus, a few words about the achievement of this narrator should be made in summary.

Stein's use of the unreliable narrator in *Ida* proves again that her narrative techniques shifted to accommodate a current interest. In *Ida* we see a fictionalization of Stein's conviction that identity is as elusive and unreliable as the narrator who tells the story. We also see the reflection of Stein's idea that the very presentation of character in the twentieth-century novel will be forever influenced by the novel's failure to compete with the communications media in the projection of personality.

In a sense Donald Sutherland is right in saying that

"*Ida* is strictly speaking no novel at all but belongs to the tradition of the philosophical farce or romance which is probably at its purest in Voltaire's *Candide*."[29] Like *Candide*, *Ida* presents a complete disregard for "believable" settings, characters, and time conceptions (or sequences); and also like *Candide*, *Ida* is primarily concerned with philosophical ideas, rather than with plot as such.

In another sense, however, Sutherland is in error. At no time in *Candide* does the narrator ever want the reader to sympathize with anything but "tending one's own garden." *Candide* is essentially negative. *Ida*, on the other hand, although it includes elements of the farcical, ends with its central figure finding a comfortable love and through it resolving her search and her long life of wandering. *Ida* is essentially a positive work.

MRS. REYNOLDS

Mrs. Reynolds[30] is Gertrude Stein's last work of fiction. It was followed immediately by her last autobiographical work, *Wars I Have Seen*.[31] Parts of the two works bear close resemblances to each other in the same way that *Everybody's Autobiography* and *Ida* resembled each other. *Mrs. Reynolds* is a fictionalization of some of the material, and the concerns, which appear in nonfictional form in *Wars I Have Seen*. (It will be recalled that *Ida* was the fictionalization, in part, of Gertrude Stein's concern about massive public treatment of her identity which she had discussed in *Everybody's Autobiography*.)

While discussion of *Mrs. Reynolds* should be limited, strictly speaking, to the narrative techniques of the work, some other aspects deserve attention because the book has not received the extensive critical examination that some of Stein's other works have.

Like *Ida, Mrs. Reynolds* is subtitled, "A Novel." And, like *Ida*, this work contains a narrator who requires close examination from a number of standpoints in order to be understood. But first, some discussion of the content of *Mrs. Reynolds* is necessary.

During the years of the Nazi invasion of France, beginning in 1940, and until the liberation of France in 1944, Gertrude Stein and Alice Toklas lived in Bilignin and then in Culoz. Because they were both from Jewish backgrounds, their friends attempted to persuade them first to leave for the United States, and when that failed, at least to sit out the war in Switzerland. The two women did neither, preferring in Stein's words, ". . . to go regularly wherever we are sent than to go irregularly where nobody can help us if we are in trouble. . . ."[32]

They stayed in France throughout the war, and Gertrude Stein wrote *Mrs. Reynolds,* and then *Wars I Have Seen* while they were virtual prisoners there.[33]

Mrs. Reynolds covers the years 1940-1942 primarily, although there are some references dating back to 1935. The story revolves around two couples, Mr. and Mrs. Reynolds, and his brother and wife, William and Hope Reynolds. Gertrude Stein wrote in the "Epilogue" to the work:

> This book is an effort to show the way anybody could feel these years. It is a perfectly ordinary couple living an ordinary life and having ordinary conversations and really not suffering personally from everything that is happening but over them, all over them is the shadow of two men, and then the shadow of one of the two men gets bigger and then blows away and there

is no other. There is nothing historical about this book except the state of mind. [267]

The "two men" Stein refers to are certainly Adolph Hitler, and probably Joseph Stalin. One must rely upon internal evidence in the work since the identity of the two men is not specifically given by the narrator. Be that as it may, these men, or their "shadows," are interesting elements in this work because, like shadows, they never actually appear in "flesh and blood." We will see how this works presently.

Like the narrator of *Three Lives,* and of *Ida,* the narrator of *Mrs. Reynolds* speaks in the same speech patterns and rhythms used by the characters. The following example shows both the narrator and the characters using apparently unrelated thoughts as if they were perfectly normal human communicative procedures.

> But when Angel Harper was forty-three there were plenty of bridges everywhere and he kept on being forty-three. It was not yet all over.
> Mrs. Reynolds said, under or over, and her husband Mr. Reynolds said let us go to bed.
> It is natural that if any one has an employee they should worry if he was run over.
> My husband Mr. Reynolds, said Mrs. Reynolds turned as pale as a lemon.
> After all said Mrs. Reynolds I like to see people I know well dressed and I like to know where they are going and what they do when they are there and how they come home again.
> I tell them I know said Mrs. Reynolds and when I tell them what I know then they tell me if it is so. And it is very nice to know said Mrs. Reynolds. Mr. Reynolds was a little tired after his shock. But he did not go to bed any earlier than was his custom. [87-88]

And another example,

> Leave carrots out put salads in were the words with which
> Mrs. Reynolds greeted some one. That some one said not at all I
> would rather not than not at all. Mrs. Reynolds began to laugh
> and then a little more and she laughed again. Then once in a
> while Mr. Reynolds came and he smiled when he went away
> and when he came again he was still smiling.
> That was a happy day, at any rate it was a happy evening. [89]

To use Stein's own words, we can see that the "state of mind" of the characters is much the same as that of the narrator. In this regard, the narrator of *Mrs. Reynolds* is similar to those of *Three Lives,* and of *Ida.*

One further resemblance between the narrator of *Ida* and of *Mrs. Reynolds* is that both are unreliable much of the time. We saw in *Ida* that the narrator was justified artistically by the unreality of the dream world projected in that book. In a sense, Mrs. Reynolds lives in an interior dream world too. Of course, her dream world is much different from Ida's, because Ida's world is not as large as Mrs. Reynolds's is; Ida's world is one of a philosophical conception of identity, while Mrs. Reynolds's world encompasses the chaos of the beginning years of the Nazi holocaust in Europe. The unreliable narrator of *Mrs. Reynolds* is, however, the unreliable narrator of a world which is interior — a "state of mind" rather than a world of reality.[34] The narrator of the following passages is the narrator of the entire book. Several examples of this narrator are given below in order to show how much a part of the work he is.

> The son could be liked by any one, not alone for he was never
> alone not drunk for he was always drunk not sober for he was
> quite often nearly sober, but just enough so that one day he was
> married. He said marrying was nobody's business but his own
> and his father never forgave him. Not that that made any dif-
> ference to any one because if he wanted to, he and his wife

could live with his father and sister, which they did. [17]

Another example,

> The widow of the tea-king had a friend, he was librarian of a
> legislative assembly. He and his wife had been married many
> years and had no children and then they had a little girl an un-
> usually pretty one. The father always said nothing. He was a
> pleasant man and said pleasant things, he said he always said it
> is a pleasure to listen. His wife was very obedient and very ac-
> tive and often went in and out, and the little girl might have
> been a grandchild, only she was not she was their daughter. [20]

In the following examples of the unreliable narrator,
the cool, quiet, unemotional tone of the voice contributes to the seeming objectivity of a narrator who is
in actual fact a profound part of the subjectivity of the
world being projected.

> She was rather hoping that she would never see a boy named
> Roger again. He had fallen and broken his hand, not seriously,
> and actually he did go away and neither Mr. nor Mrs. Reynolds
> ever saw him again.
> This was not quite so, Mr. Reynolds did see him again but this
> was of no importance to any one. [41]

An additional example of this voice is the following,

> When Mrs. Reynolds did not know, her teeth hurt her, and her
> teeth hurt her then. Some one told her that Angel Harper could
> be angry. Perhaps he will be drowned said Mrs. Reynolds
> hopefully. . . .
> Mrs. Reynolds was very patient and she was never angry but
> she did think that anybody who was angry should be drowned
> should be drowned dead in water. She did not say it of Angel
> Harper because she never mentioned Angel Harper. [49]

And a final example,

> Far away and every day Joseph Lane made hay. He likes to
> make hay in a beard and in time, and in more than appalling

sickness. But little by little fire goes away. That is what Joseph Lane says to his son but he never sees his son so he cannot say to him what he does say to him. [101]

However, the similarities between the narrator of *Mrs. Reynolds* and those of *Three Lives* and *Ida* end with the suggestion that they are reflections of speech patterns and projections of interior worlds, in some cases.

The narrator of *Mrs. Reynolds* has some dimensions that Stein's other narrators do not have. We suggested previously that this narrator is "usually a third person." That unconventional term is used because this narrator appears as a third-person narrator at the very beginning of the book; then, by the third page, he has become a first-person narrator; then he appears to return to the third-person form, but in fact, the distance between the narrator and the author, having been established in the reader's mind by the single use of first person, is somehow never confused by the reader again.

The work begins with an apparent third-person narrator.

It takes courage to be courageous said Mrs. Reynolds.
She said it used to be Sunday and now it was Tuesday.
If it were Sunday and Tuesday, well it would be a day too much.
Mrs. Reynolds never sighed, she sometimes cried but she never sighed.
All the world knows how to cry but not all the world knows how to sigh.
Sighing is extra.
Mrs. Reynolds was a pretty woman and she had never been unwell.
Her husband was a nice man he looked nice and he was nice.
He was not well and strong but he could get along very well.

They were a good-looking couple and they had begun life and were going along. They had gone along. [1]

This narrator appears to be conversational, if a bit cryptic at times. The conversational tone of his voice lends a special credence to the sudden appearance of the first person two pages later.

This had nothing to do with Mrs. Reynolds having been born on Tuesday, she knew that there was nothing to do, the stars had arranged it that she was to be born on a Tuesday. Nothing could stop it and she was born on a Tuesday.

She was sure that the stars had so arranged it and that there was nothing possible but that, she believed it and so do I. [3]

This last sentence is one of the very few times in the entire book in which the narrator uses the first person — hence the qualification of the narrator as usually third person. However, the combination of the conversational tone of voice with this occurrence of the first person creates for the reader the closeness to the material and characters which the first person often affords, and yet the unreliability of the narrator forces the reader to recognize that there is a distance between the narrator and the author. Once again, as in the case of *The Autobiography of Alice B. Toklas*, we see Stein having her cake and eating it too. In *The Autobiography of Alice B. Toklas* we saw Stein utilizing all of the advantages of the first-person narrator while suffering none of its usual disadvantages, simply because she ignored the disadvantages; in *Mrs. Reynolds* we see a narrator who draws the reader (or perhaps lulls him) into a sense of credulity by his conversational tone and his reference to the first person, only to snap the reader's mind, at will, back to a sense of the dream world through the very *unreliability* of the narrator.

161

This is not the only singularity in *Mrs. Reynolds.* The organization of this work is different from anything else we have seen Stein undertake. It will be recalled that Gertrude Stein once said that in any writing there should "not be a sense of time, but an existence suspended in time." *Mrs. Reynolds* marks a departure from this philosophy — it is developed around a highly organized, although most idiosyncratic, sense of time. This departure is the great distinction and accomplishment of the work compared to other Stein works.

The book exhibits a considerable amount of tension — achieved by the balance of two modes of time: the historical versus the prophetic. These two strict temporalities are pitted against each other in such a way that we perceive the rise of the two "historical" shadows, Adolph Hitler and Joseph Stalin, played against the prophecy (by Saint Odile) that both shadows would fall.

Certainly Angel Harper is Adolph Hitler. He is the "stronger shadow" Stein referred to in her "Epilogue." Angel Harper is an acronym for Adolph Hitler, that much is obvious. But there are several other interesting clues to his identity in the work. First, and also quite obvious, is the fact that Angel Harper is referred to as a "dictator" several times, including a reference to Angel Harper's having brought everyone to war (33).

It is in the choice of the name itself, not alone in the initials, that much of the interest of this character lies. Mrs. Reynolds discussed the coming of Anti-Christ (43) with her neighbors. To many Christians, Adolph Hitler was the Anti-Christ of the twentieth century. In traditional Christianity the original devil, or Anti-Christ, was a fallen Angel — thus the name "Angel" for

"Adolph." That Stein actually intended such a comparison can be seen in the more direct reference, "If blonde people brush their hair, and make it curl they are called Gabriel. If dark people brush their hair and it does not curl, they are called Angel Harper" (44). (The ironies implicit in the choice, by a Jew who lived through World War II, of the name Angel for Adolph will not be lost on any reader.)

Much the same reasoning could apply to the choice of the last name "Harper," for Hitler. As a noun, a harp is played, traditionally, by an angel. An angel is a harper. But, as a verb, harp means to dwell tiresomely on the same subject — in this case war, persecution, and general chaos. In this case, harper, then, not only carries the root word "harp," which is associated with angels, but also serves to make us aware that this angel, the Anti-Christ, is a harper of destruction. And, of course, this angel "harps" while the world burns.

That Stein intended Joseph Lane to be Joseph Stalin, the second shadow of her epilogue, can be inferred from the text. Stein did not do as much playing with the name, excepting that the first names are identical, as she did with Angel Harper/Adolph Hitler. The evidence that Joseph Lane is Joseph Stalin begins to mount, of course, with the historical knowledge that the two shadows hanging over Europe during those years were, in fact, Hitler and Stalin. And for the French people in 1940-1942 the shadow of the Russian dictator (Stein refers to Lane as a "dictator") was linked with that of the German dictator by the 1940 alliance between Germany and Russia.[35] Subsequently, of course, when Hitler invaded Russia, the shadow of the second man, Stalin, became less ominous to the French.[36]

163

Pitted against these two historical shadows are several minor, and one major, prophecy. *Mrs. Reynolds* is divided into thirteen parts — each roughly about twenty pages in length. The first hundred pages, or so, deal with the time before Angel Harper became such an ominous force in the lives of Mrs. Reynolds and her husband and neighbors. This part of the work includes the minor prophecies. For example, a musician who "neither played nor sang nor composed" (12), prophesies, when Mrs. Reynolds is a little girl, that she will someday become Mrs. Reynolds. That prophecy comes true. Then, a judge, who keeps a little book entitled "Intentions and Predictions" (18) predicts several things about her, which also come true.

Mrs. Reynolds, herself, makes several predictions. She predicts the war-time food shortage to come: "Mrs. Reynolds the wife of Mr. Reynolds stayed at home and breathed out a sigh.[37] She liked to prophesy. She said, purchase bye and bye will be not a matter of money but a matter of personality. If you are popular you can buy if you are not popular you can die" (22).

However, the major prediction, upon which rests the major element in the time organization of this novel, is made by a saint — Saint Odile. The narrator says, "Mrs. Reynolds liked holiness but only holiness if it is accompanied by predictions. Holiness often is" (22).

Gertrude Stein had a long-time interest in saints. She wrote *Four Saints in Three Acts* in 1927, and she and Alice Toklas never seemed to tire of visiting religious places and investigating "local" saints.[38] (She admired saints, in wonderfully Steinesque fashion, because "they stand around and do nothing.")[39]

The prediction of Saint Odile is a lengthy and recurring one in *Mrs. Reynolds,* but in essence she predicted (according to Stein), in the seventh century, that the Germans would begin a terrible war, and after some horrifying successes, would be defeated.[40] This is the prophecy against which the rise of Angel Harper and Joseph Lane is played in the book.

Mrs. Reynolds believes completely in the prediction that Angel Harper will be defeated. This belief keeps her morale up during the darkest days of the war.[41]

So far we have been discussing the tension created in this novel by the juxtaposition of some fairly weighty historical fact. However, the narrator in *Mrs. Reynolds* presents this historical material in language which has earned its freedom.

The following passage is an example of language at play in presenting the shadowy nuances of the "facts" of history.[42] The paragraph presages Hitler's defeat in Russia:

Angel Harper knew that when he was fourteen he first knew that there was an enormous moon a cold moon that came up not too soon but not at noon but at night, and it was an enormous moon and a cold moon although spring had come, and the moon was called a red moon a rough moon a Russian moon and Angel Harper knew that when he had been fourteen he had first seen this moon to know it as such a moon and now Angel Harper was fifty-two and spring was come and it was true, the big moon the enormous moon the cold moon the red moon the rough moon the Russian moon was a moon. Angel Harper hoped it might be noon, but was it noon, no said Angel Harper and he hoped it was yesterday but no it was not yesterday it was today, and Angel Harper could not go away. [207-08]

Surely this is the very antithesis of what we take to be "historical" treatment. The defeat of Adolph Hitler by Joseph Stalin has been totally denuded of the sense of time in the paragraph. Note also the constant play of rhyme. It not only makes the fixed historical identity of Angel Harper irrelevant, problematic, and weirdly human, but it also undermines or ignores the weight of history as a matter of frozen record: "A cold moon that came up not too soon but not at noon." The phrase strips the weight from the historical event, but in some ways it encircles the *nature* of the historical fact that Hitler was defeated by the Russians. The technique is one of high distillation, in which all irrelevancies of time, place, emotion, or even cultural attitudes, have been stripped away. The passage itself contains hauntingly beautiful alliteration which also serves to place the historical incident on an equal par with the concept of autotelic language. ". . . and the moon was called a red moon a rough moon a Russian moon."

The approach is even more startling when it is applied to another tensional device — Angel Harper's age. His age is used throughout the book as a reminder of Saint Odile's prophecy that he will fall. Constant references to Angel Harper's age reflect either the hope that he will not live to have another birthday, or the despair because he has. (The device is not unlike that in *Catch-22* in which the men are constantly being told that their number of missions will be limited, and then that they must surpass that number.) Note the play of rhyme in the following:

> Angel Harper was forty-six.
> Exactly forty-six.
> Really when Angel Harper was forty-six he was in a fix. And so was any one. And every one. Believe it or not it is true and it made every one pretty blue. [100]

The narrator continues some time later, ". . . and in the silence Angel Harper was forty-six. Forty-six was there and all of it was on the edge. Edge of what, nobody asked but it was an edge. It was the edge of forty-seven Angel Harper was forty-seven" (104).

Gertrude Stein was a Jew in occupied France at the time when all Jews there lived under the constant threat of the concentration camp. And her narrator says, ". . . when Angel Harper was forty-six he was in a fix. And so was any one. . . ." It is an "unhistorical" use of language, to say the least,[43] and that is the very point. To present a work dealing with the most important historical event of our time through an experimental medium freely playing with its own generative powers is in itself daringly innovative. But to counterpoint such a work with notations of a most familiar "historical" theme — the passing of time signalled by birthdays — and to orchestrate the whole into a sort of dreaming memory-life of the fantastic yet historical protagonist is the sort of virtuoso performance which Stein is at last able to accomplish.[44] The work ends on the note, "Angel Harper was not fifty-five alive."

Throughout Stein's experimentation in her return to the narrative form she was concerned with the way in which any author represents time, without being false to it. In her autobiographical works she concentrated on the difficulties of "remembering yourself," and of "believing yourself," when you have remembered. During the writing of the autobiographical works she tried one kind of narrator after another in her determination to conquer the tyranny of time. In *The Autobiography of Alice B. Toklas* she sought to "remember" through someone else's eyes. In *Everybody's*

Autobiography, written much closer to the time "remembered" than *The Autobiography of Alice B. Toklas*, she tried to suspend time through the use of the run-on sentence and the durational voice in narration.[45] The nonautobiographical work *Ida* carries her concern with identity into a fictionalized form. In that work Stein is concerned with identity and how the individual is to separate her private and her public identities. The narrator plays with time concepts in these terms with phrases like, "One day it was before or after," in order to draw the parallel between identity and remembering: remembering is interwoven with time and both are elusive and unreliable. But it is in *Mrs. Reynolds* that Gertrude Stein set for herself the most difficult challenge in her struggle to master time. In dealing with perhaps the most time-oriented of all human concepts, history and prophecy, by stripping them of everything but their "existence suspended in time," and by letting her language play through and around them, she brought to the problems a new and illuminating perception.

NOTES

1 Gertrude Stein, "A Transatlantic Interview," in *Gertrude Stein: A Primer for the Gradual Understanding of Gertrude Stein*, ed. Robert B. Haas (Los Angeles: Black Sparrow Press, 1971), p. 20.

2 Gertrude Stein, *The Autobiography of Alice B. Toklas* (New York: Harcourt, Brace, 1933).

3 John Brinnin, *The Third Rose: Gertrude Stein and Her World* (Boston: Little, Brown, 1959), pp. 209-11, reports that part of the original manuscript of the book at the Yale University library is written in Toklas's handwriting. He does not actually suggest that this indicates that Toklas wrote her own autobiography while

Gertrude Stein took the credit for it, but he does suggest it is a possibility, although "sufficiently heretical that no one has dared advance it directly" (209). Since Toklas was Stein's secretary, typist, and proofreader for the twenty-five years preceding this work, her handwriting on Stein's manuscripts is not very provocative evidence.

4 They are: "Two: Gertrude Stein and Her Brother"; *The Autobiography of Alice B. Toklas; Everybody's Autobiography; Paris France;* and *Wars I Have Seen.*

5 Gertrude Stein wrote *Four Saints in Three Acts An Opera To Be Sung* in 1927. Virgil Thomson wrote the music to it; and it was first performed in Hartford, Connecticut, during Stein's lecture tour in America in 1935.

6 Stein, "A Transatlantic Interview," p. 19.

7 There are probably at least two reasons for this: the work is centered around the importance of Stein, and therefore is not really concerned with more than the surface facts of Toklas's previous existence; and also these early years were covered to some extent in the portrait, "Ada," already discussed.

8 Alice Toklas was born in San Francisco on April 30, 1877.

9 Gertrude Stein was born in Allegheny, Pennsylvania, on February 3, 1874.

10 One of the many titles originally considered for this work was *My Twenty-five Years With Gertrude Stein.* See *The Autobiography of Alice B. Toklas,* p. 309.

11 I am indebted to Wayne Booth, *The Rhetoric of Fiction* (Chicago: University of Chicago Press, 1966), for the discussion of this term.

12 Robert Bartlett Haas, "Another Garland for Gertrude Stein," *What Are Masterpieces* (New York: Pitman, 1970), p. 14.

13 Brinnin, *The Third Rose,* p. 307.

14 Gertrude Stein, *Everybody's Autobiography* (New York: Random House, 1937).

15 Stein, *Everybody's Autobiography,* p. 8.

16 Leo Stein presents *his* view of his relationship with his sister in his fascinating collection of letters and occasional thoughts entitled *Journey Into the Self,* ed. Edmund Fuller (New York: Crown, 1950). The following is an excerpt of a letter he wrote to Mabel Weeks on February 7, 1913. The attitudes reflected in this letter did not change throughout his life.

One of the greatest changes that has become decisive in recent times is the fairly definite 'disaggregation' of Gertrude and myself. The presence of Alice was a godsend, as it enabled the thing to happen without any explosion. As we have come to maturity, we have come to find that there is practically nothing under the heavens that we don't either disagree about, or at least regard with different sympathies. The crucial thing of course is our work. In my case this is of comparatively little importance because in the first place I never suspected Gertrude of having any interest in the criticism of ideas, and in the second place I have no desire for glory. I want to be right of course, but I'm fairly well satisfied if I'm convinced of that myself, and I want those ideas which I believe to be right to prevail, but I don't care in the least who makes them prevail and gets any reward that attaches thereto. Gertrude on the other hand hungers and thirsts for *gloire,* and it was of course a serious thing for her that I can't abide her stuff and think it abominable. This would not have been so bad if there had been any general recognition without; a prophet can support not being honored in his own country when other lands sufficiently acclaim him, but when the acclamation otherwhere is faint the absence of support at home is painful. To this has been added my utter refusal to accept the later phases of Picasso with whose tendency Gertrude has so closely allied herself. They both seem to me entirely on the wrong track. Picasso is to my belief an illustrator by his gifts, one of the greatest who was ever born, but illustration in our day is anathema and he wants to be the creator of a great and original form. Gertrude by long and careful systematic study has gotten to have an enormous knowledge of individuals and of individuals in their individual relations. I have often been struck by her extraordinary incapacity to understand the personality of politicians and others in their larger social relations. Her artistic capacity is, I think, extremely small. I have just been looking over the Melanctha thing again. Gertrude's mind is about as little nimble as a mind can be. She can only express herself by elaborately telling all at full length. The grammar and vocabulary and sentence structure of the three lives might have been different in a dozen ways without loss, provided she had put down all she knows about the people concerned. It is the insistence on the facts that makes, to my thinking, the significance of the book. Well, Gertrude also wants to create a great and original form. I can't understand the *Portrait of Mabel Dodge,* but none the less I feel that I am not exceeding my reasonable privilege in thinking it damned nonsense. A portrait of a person that I know pretty intimately which conveys absolutely nothing to me, a far from inexperienced reader with no prejudices in the matter, seems to me to have something the matter with it. (I've tried to read the darned thing a number of times.) And Gertrude prides herself particularly on her wonderful rhythm of prose and can do things like 'There was not that velvet spread when there was a pleasant head.' The iteration and reiteration of those lines is in the main factual, and though it doesn't make me happy I can feel its force, but since then she has developed iteration as a stylistic device and there I halt. The *Portrait of Mabel Dodge* was directly inspired by Picasso's latest form. The last time but one that Picasso and I talked about art, he said that once upon a time he had thought that an artist should be an animal with a talent, like Renoir, and should just go ahead and paint, but now he had changed his mind and felt that an artist should use his intelligence to develop his art. Picasso is a man of the finest sensitiveness, the keenest observation and a strong sense of man in his humors. Goethe said of Byron that he was a child when he thought, but Pablo is then a babe in arms. Both he and Gertrude are using their intellects, which they ain't got, to do what would need the finest critical tact, which they ain't got neither, and they are in my belief turning out the most Godalmighty rubbish that is to be found. [52-53]

17 For a complete presentation of Gertrude Stein's view of punctuation, see Gertrude Stein, "Poetry and Grammar," *Lectures in America* (New York: Random House, 1935), pp. 209-46.

18 Gertrude Stein, "And Now . . . ," *Vanity Fair* 43 (September 1934):35, 65.

19 Donald Sutherland, *Gertrude Stein: A Biography of Her Work* (New Haven: Yale University Press, 1951), p. 153.

20 Preoccupation with this idea recurs throughout Gertrude Stein's later works. Apparently it was important enough to her philosophically that it has been recorded by Alice Toklas (In *What is Remembered* [New York: Rinehart and Winston, 1963], p. 173), as Gertrude Stein's last words. The incident appears thusly, and is the last paragraph in the book:

> By this time Gertrude Stein was in a sad state of indecision and worry. I sat next to her and she said to me early in the afternoon, What is the answer? I was silent. In that case, she said, what is the question? Then the whole afternoon was troubled, confused and very uncertain, and later in the afternoon they took her away on a wheeled stretcher to the operating room and I never saw her again.

21 It cannot be overlooked that this very simplicity is what has led a critic such as Wyndham Lewis to term it "a faux-naif," in, *Time and Western Man* (Boston: Beacon Press, 1957), p. xi. Lewis describes what he terms the "child personality of Miss Stein," elsewhere in the book (62-63). The argument it seems to me reflects more of Lewis's pathological condescension toward other successful writers than it does his critical acumen.

22 Although all autobiography may strive for this effect, all autobiography does not, as a matter of course, succeed. Perhaps one should say rather that all *good* autobiography obtains it. A case in point is the autobiography of Albert Speer, Hitler's industrial genius, *Inside the Third Reich* (New York: Macmillan Company, 1970). This autobiography is deeply flawed by Speer's selection of only that detail from his life which demonstrates that he did not know how evil Hitler's regime really was, although he (Speer) was terribly sorry it all happened. As a result, the reader gets little that is really credible about the man Albert Speer, although, interestingly enough, one gets "perhaps the best portrait of Adolph Hitler the world will ever have," as James O'Donnell of the *New York Times Magazine* has said.

23 Gertrude Stein, *Ida* (New York: Random House, 1941). The work was written in 1937, directly after the writing of *Everybody's Autobiography*. See Robert B. Haas and Donald C. Gallup, *A Catalogue of the Published and Unpublished Writings of Gertrude Stein* (New Haven: Yale University Press, 1941), p. 55.

24 Bilignin is in the south of France. Stein and Toklas spent their summers there, and part of *Everybody's Autobiography* was written there.

25 *Everybody's Autobiography* ends with the sentence, ". . . perhaps I am not I even if my little dog knows me but anyway I like what I have and now it is today" (318).

26 Stein, "A Transatlantic Interview," p. 22.

27 Brinnin, *The Third Rose*, p. 360, writes,

> . . . *Ida* is the story of a woman whose mere being is more important than anything she does or might think of doing, simply because she is Ida, the dream girl made flesh. Existing not only in the dreams of others but in a dream of herself. . . .

28 Gertrude Stein had actually witnessed a real walking marathon in Chicago during her lecture tour there. The incident is described in *Everybody's Autobiography*, p. 209.

29 Sutherland, *Gertrude Stein*, p. 154.

30 Gertrude Stein, *Mrs. Reynolds and Five Earlier Novelettes* (New Haven: Yale University Press, 1952). Internal evidence indicates that the book was written during the years 1940-1942, as the Yale edition states. However, Haas and Gallup, *A Catalogue of the Published and Unpublished Writings*, p. 55, list the work as completed in 1941.

31 Gertrude Stein, *Wars I Have Seen* (New York: Random House, 1945).

32 *Ibid.*, p. 50. The description of what Stein called "those difficult moments" covers pages 49-51 of this work.

33 See Stein, *Wars I Have Seen* (especially pages 145-48), for a description of the "terror of the Germans all about us," and the

fact that Stein and Toklas did not dare "go out" during those times.

34 Gertrude Stein wrote, in *Wars I Have Seen,* p. 44: ". . . realism was the last thing the nineteenth century did completely. Anybody can understand that there is no point in being realistic about here and now . . . there is no realism now [June 1943], life is not real it is not earnest, it is strange which is an entirely different matter."

35 For a thorough discussion of the complexities of those times in French politics, see William L. Shirer, *The Collapse of the Third Republic: An Inquiry Into the Fall of France in 1940* (New York: Simon and Schuster, 1969).

36 This idea is not so simple as it appears here. During the First World War, the French had great hopes from the "great Russian steam roller" — see Barbara Tuchman, *The Guns of August* (New York: Macmillan, 1962), pp. 75-87. When that steam roller never materialized, French hopes turned to fear of the rising Communist regime in Russia. When Hitler signed the alliance with Russia in 1940, these fears spread among the middle and upper classes in France. (See Shirer, *The Collapse of the Third Republic* [New York: Simon and Schuster, 1969].) Shirer contends that when Hitler invaded Russia, the French population was terribly split by Monarchists who favored Hitler because of their fear of Communists in France, and by the French peasantry who were sympathetic to the Communist cause. He also contends that it was Stalin who gave the word first to cooperate with the Germans, when Stalin and Hitler were allies, then to resist through the French underground after Hitler invaded Russia. At any rate, the political scene in France at the time was very confused and divided.

37 The fact that Mrs. Reynolds breathed out a sigh is another interesting example of the unreliable narrator. We were told on page 1 that Mrs. Reynolds "never sighed."

38 In *What is Remembered,* pp. 68-71, Alice Toklas describes the long hours she and Stein used to spend in such activity.

39 Stein, *Everybody's Autobiography,* p. 109.

40 As the mention of Saint Odile is made some fifty times in *Mrs. Reynolds* it is difficult to present the entire prediction in the text of this book. However, the prediction, along with a discussion of how Gertrude Stein happened to use this particular saint in this book, is discussed in *Wars I Have Seen*, pp. 57-68. As this work is autobiographical, and not fiction, there is no reason to believe that the account of Saint Odile's predictions in *Wars I Have Seen* is not actually the way it happened. The following is taken from Stein's account of it in *Wars I Have Seen*.

> In 1940 when we were all filled with sorrow and despair and a little hope and a complete certainty that after all, the Germans were not going to win . . . we had to have the prophecies of Saint Odile. . . . Saint Odile said that Germany would conquer the world would be drowned in blood and tears, and fire would be thrown from the sky upon the earth beneath and everybody would say that nothing could defeat the power and force of that army and everybody would say let us have peace at any price rather than go on suffering and then Germany at the height of its power would throw themselves against a mountain, a holy mountain, that certainly was Moscow because in the time of Saint Odile Moscow was a city of convents and was called the holy mountain and from then on there would be a weakening . . . and then would come fighting in the streets of the city of cities in the citadel of citadels . . . and then there would be the beginning of the real end of Germany . . . we have all been cherishing copies of this prophecy ever since 1940, and . . . there is a copy in Latin of the original prophecy in Lyon, which one of the young seminarists at Belley translated for me into French. . . .

41 Stein, *Wars I Have Seen*, p. 60. Stein wrote about the prophecy and her own morale: "And this was a comfort so often a comfort and it is a comfort again, like a road you find on the map and then see in real life. . . ."

42 For a differently oriented experimentation in presenting such nuances, see Rainer Maria Rilke, *The Notebooks of Malte Laurids Brigge*, trans. M. D. Herter (New York: Norton Library, 1964).

43 It is interesting to note that another great work of art dealing

with Hitler (and history) in what critics considered an "un-historical" manner appeared circa 1940. It was Charlie Chaplin's brilliant but misapprehended movie, *The Great Dictator*. In it, Chaplin, himself a Jew, juxtaposed the brutality and terrorism of the Nazis with what seemed to critics to be the lighthearted "tramp" image that had made Chaplin so famous. In a memorable scene from this movie, several Nazi "toughs" have smashed the windows and written "Jew" in red paint on the front of the shop owned by a barber (played by Chaplin). The audience expects the barber to become terrified and try to escape the nightmare — which was being enacted all over Europe at the time. Instead, Chaplin, doing a little tap dance, simply wipes away the paint in time to the music he is whistling — winking and smiling all the while at the Nazis.

Chaplin was viciously attacked by the critics of the time for being "frivolous," and for "failing" to see the "weight" of the tragic events. Indeed the criticism was so violent that the movie has still not been reshown in the USA (except in isolated "art" movie houses), even though it is a masterpiece.

It is not unlikely that *Mrs. Reynolds* would have suffered the same critical reception had it been published when it was first written in 1942.

44 I am indebted to Professor Gayatri C. Spivak for the discussion of this idea.

45 Gertrude Stein retained this narrative voice in the last two autobiographical works she wrote: *Paris France*, and *Wars I have Seen*.

Language, Time,
Gertrude Stein & Us

We have been examining a writer whose forty-two-year career was a constant experiment. Writers who preceded Gertrude Stein, and many who have followed, have often been concerned with creating works of art which reflect either the writer's interpretation of subjective reality, or his/her understanding of objective reality. Gertrude Stein's career reflected these concerns too, but as she matured as an artist she became more and more preoccupied with the power of language itself to create a reality beyond the subjective or the objective vision of the creating artist. Concurrent with her interest in the self-generative powers of language was her interest in that other reality, time, which absorbed her especially during the last phase of her career.

As Gertrude Stein's interests in various areas of experimentation changed, her use of the narrator as a device also shifted to accommodate those changes. In the early days of her career we saw a rapid progression from the objective, third-person narrator of *Q.E.D.*, to the narrator of *Three Lives* who appears to be a reflection of the characters themselves; then to the narrator of the early portraits who had almost disappeared in favor of self-generative language. With the writing of *Tender Buttons,* which has been marked as the beginning of Stein's middle period, the interest in nonrepresentational language, already in embryonic form at the end of her early years, became the dominant interest. This interest lasted about twenty years and in turn gave way to another direction, also visible in embryonic form in the middle period: the narrative form which reflects a sense of liquid time.

Gertrude Stein wrote more than five-hundred separate titles. Only a very few have been examined here in the hope of indicating a rational basis for further consideration of her vast corpus. Like so many artists who attempt to create in a new system of values, Gertrude Stein has been judged primarily under the strictures of the old system. She has suffered either from neglect or dismissal on the facile grounds that she is "inaccessible," or from ridicule based on the insistence that her works be forced into the dated confines of an Aristotelian criticism which simply does not apply to her works. She has not been given a latitude of critical judgment which would allow her work to exist within its own system of values. In brief, Gertrude Stein has not been read on her own terms.

In no way is this intended as an exhaustive study of the artistry of Gertrude Stein. It is only an attempt to indicate that she was not simply the Mother Superior of a Parisian art salon at the turn of the century. She was an important experimental writer who deserves better than she has received from critical analysis.

Bibliography

PRIMARY SOURCES
Books

Stein, Gertrude. *The Autobiography of Alice B. Toklas.* New York: Harcourt Brace, 1933.

——. *Everybody's Autobiography.* New York: Random House, 1937.

——. *Fernhurst, Q.E.D., and Other Early Writings* [by] GERTRUDE STEIN. Edited by Leon Katz. New York: Liveright, 1971.

——. *The Geographical History of America.* New York: Vintage Books, 1973.

——. *Geography and Plays.* Boston: Four Seas, 1922.

——. *How Writing is Written. Volume II of the Previously Uncollected Writings of Gertrude Stein.* Edited by Robert Bartlett Haas. Los Angeles: Black Sparrow Press, 1974.

——. *Ida, A Novel.* New York: Random House, 1941.

——. *Lectures in America.* New York: Random House, 1935.

——. *Lucy Church Amiably.* Paris: Plain Edition, 1930.

——. *The Making of Americans.* New York: Harcourt Brace, 1934.

——. *Mrs. Reynolds and Five Earlier Novelettes.* New Haven: Yale University Press, 1952.

——. *Paris France.* London: B. T. Batsford, 1940.

——. *Portraits and Prayers.* New York: Random House, 1934.

——. *Reflections on the Atom Bomb. Volume I of the Previously Uncollected Writings of Gertrude Stein.* Edited by Robert Bartlett

Haas. Los Angeles: Black Sparrow Press, 1974.

___. *Selected Writings of Gertrude Stein.* Edited by Carl Van Vechten. New York: Vintage Books, 1972.

___. *Tender Buttons.* New York: Claire Marie Press, 1914.

___. *Things As They Are.* Vermont: Pawlet Press, 1950.

___. *Three Lives.* New York: Modern Library, 1933.

___. "A Transatlantic Interview: 1946." *Gertrude Stein: A Primer for the Gradual Understanding of Gertrude Stein.* Edited by Robert B. Haas. Los Angeles: Black Sparrow Press, 1971.

___. *Two and Other Early Portraits.* New Haven: Yale University Press, 1951.

___. *Wars I Have Seen.* New York: Random House, 1945.

___. *What Are Masterpieces.* Edited by Robert B. Haas. New York: Pitman, 1970.

Articles

Stein, Gertrude. "And Now. . . ." *Vanity Fair* 43 (1934):35, 65.

___. "J. H. Jane Heap." *Little Review* 12 (1929):9-10.

___. "Made a Mile Away." *Transition* 8 (1927):155-65.

___. "Vacation in Britany." *Little Review* 8 (1922):5-6. Reprinted by permission of Calman A. Levin, The Offices of Daniel C. Joseph, administrator of the estate of Gertrude Stein.

SECONDARY SOURCES

Books

Aldrich, Mildred. *A Hilltop on the Marne.* Boston: Houghton Mifflin, 1917.

___. *On the Edge of the War Zone.* Cambridge: Cambridge University Press, 1917.

Apollinaire, Guillaume. *The Cubist Painters: Aesthetic Meditations.* Translated by Lionel Abel. New York: Wittenborn, Schultz, 1949.

Bergson, Henri. *Creative Evolution.* Translated by Arthur Mitchell. New York: Modern Library, 1944.

___. *Time and Free Will: An Essay on the Immediate Data of Consciousness.* Translated by F. L. Pogson. New York: Macmillan, 1928.

Booth, Wayne. *The Rhetoric of Fiction.* Chicago: University of Chicago Press, 1966.

Bridgman, Richard. *Gertrude Stein in Pieces.* New York: Oxford University Press, 1970.

Brinnin, John Malcolm. *The Third Rose: Gertrude Stein and Her World.* Boston: Little, Brown, 1959.

Cézanne, Paul. *Letters.* Edited by John Rewald. Translated by Marguerite Kay. London: Bruno Cassirer, 1941.

Cowley, Malcolm. *Exile's Return.* New York: Viking Press, 1962.

Dickinson, Emily. *Poems by Emily Dickinson.* Edited by Martha Dickinson Bianchi and Alfred Leete Hampson. Boston: Little, Brown, 1942.

Flaubert, Gustave. *The Works of Gustave Flaubert.* New York: Walter J. Black, 1904.

Fry, Roger. *Cézanne: A Study of His Development.* New York: Macmillan, 1927.

Greene, Robert W. *The Poetic Theory of Pierre Reverdy.* Berkeley: University of California Press, 1967.

Haas, Robert B., and Gallup, Donald C. *A Catalogue of the Published and Unpublished Writings of Gertrude Stein.* New Haven: Yale University Press, 1941.

Hoffman, Michael J. *The Development of Abstractionism in the Writings of Gertrude Stein.* Philadelphia: University of Pennsylvania Press, 1965.

James, Henry. *The Wings of the Dove.* New York: Modern Library, 1937.

Lemaitre, Georges. *From Cubism to Surrealism in French Literature.* New York: Russell and Russell, 1967.

Lewis, Wyndham. *Time and Western Man.* Boston: Beacon Press, 1957.

Lubbock, Percy. *The Craft of Fiction.* New York: Peter Smith, 1947.

Mackworth, Cecily. *Guillaume Apollinaire and the Cubist Life.* New York: Horizon Press, 1963.

Mallarmé, Stéphane. *Mallarmé.* Edited and translated by Anthony Hartley. Baltimore: Penguin Books, 1965.

Meyerowitz, Patricia, ed. *Gertrude Stein: Writings and Lectures, 1911-1945.* London: Peter Owen, 1967.

Miller, Rosalind. *Gertrude Stein: Form and Intelligibility.* New York:

Exposition Press, 1949.

Raymond, Marcel. *From Baudelaire to Surrealism*. London: Methuen, 1970.

Rilke, Rainer Maria. *The Notebooks of Malte Laurids Brigge*. Translated by M. D. Herter. New York: Norton Library, 1964.

Scholes, Robert, and Kellogg, Robert. *The Nature of Narrative*. New York: Oxford University Press, 1966.

Shirer, William L. *The Collapse of the Third Republic: An Inquiry Into the Fall of France in 1940*. New York: Simon and Schuster, 1969.

Sitwell, Edith. *Aspects of Modern Poetry*. London: Duckworth, 1934.

Speer, Albert. *Inside the Third Reich*. New York: Macmillan, 1970.

Sprigge, Elizabeth. *Gertrude Stein: Her Life and Work*. London: Hamish Hamilton, 1957.

Stein, Leo. *Journey Into the Self*. Edited by Edmund Fuller. New York: Crown, 1950.

Stewart, Allegra. *Gertrude Stein and the Present*. Cambridge: Harvard University Press, 1967.

Sutherland, Donald. *Gertrude Stein: A Biography of Her Work*. New Haven: Yale University Press, 1951.

Toklas, Alice B. *What is Remembered*. New York: Rinehart and Winston, 1963.

Tuchman, Barbara. *The Guns of August*. New York: Macmillan, 1962.

White, Ray Lewis, ed. *Sherwood Anderson/Gertrude Stein, Correspondence and Personal Essays*. Chapel Hill: University of North Carolina Press, 1972.

Williams, William Carlos. *The Autobiography of William Carlos Williams*. New York: Random House, 1951.

Wilson, Edmund. *Axel's Castle*. New York: Charles Scribner's Sons, 1945.

Articles

Bridgman, Richard. "Melanctha." *American Literature* 33 (1961):350-59.

Dodge, Mabel. "Speculations." *Camera Work,* Special Number (June, 1913):6-9.

Stewart, Allegra. "The Quality of Gertrude Stein's Creativity." *Bibliography of American Literature* 28 (1957):488-506.

Text and display types are Palatino. Frontispiece photo courtesy of The Bettmann Archive Inc., 136 East 57th Street, New York, 10022.